A COMPREHENSIVE

BATH

ENGLAND

Discover the Rich History, culture, cuisines, Stunning Architecture, and Relaxing Thermal Spas of this Picturesque City.

Annie J. Larsen

TABLE OF CONTENT

PREFACE

Welcome to "A Comprehensive Guide to Bath, England: Discover the Rich History, Culture, Cuisines, Stunning Architecture, and Relaxing Thermal Spas of this Picturesque City." This guidebook is a testament to the extraordinary allure of Bath, a city that captivates the hearts and minds of all who visit.

Bath, situated in the beautiful county of Somerset, is where time seems to stand still, yet vibrant stories of the past come to life at every turn. This guide will take you on a fascinating journey through this enchanting city's winding streets and cobbled lanes, where ancient Roman history intertwines seamlessly with Georgian elegance.

Immerse yourself in the rich history of Bath as we delve into its origins. Discover how the Romans, recognizing the healing properties of the city's natural thermal springs, established Aquae Sulis here almost two thousand years ago. Unearth the secrets of the magnificent Roman Baths, where you can still witness the steam rising from the sacred waters that have drawn visitors for centuries.

As you stroll along Bath's Georgian crescents and terraces, you'll be transported back to the elegant era of Jane Austen. Experience the architectural wonders of the Royal Crescent, the Circus, and the Pulteney Bridge, marveling at the grandeur and symmetry that make Bath a UNESCO World Heritage site. Learn about the visionary architect John Wood, whose innovative designs shaped the city's distinctive character.

In addition to its historical charm, Bath boasts a vibrant cultural scene that continues to flourish. From the Theatre Royal, a beacon of performing arts, to the Jane Austen Centre, where the literary genius of one of England's most beloved authors is celebrated, Bath offers many cultural experiences for every visitor.

Indulge your taste buds with the culinary delights that Bath has to offer. Bath's gastronomic scene will leave you craving more, from traditional afternoon tea in elegant tea rooms to delectable local cuisines in award-winning restaurants. Explore the bustling farmers' markets, where you can sample artisanal cheeses, locally sourced produce, and exquisite handmade chocolates.

As you wander through Bath's streets, you'll find an abundance of quaint boutiques, independent shops, and artisanal craft stores. Unearth unique treasures and handmade keepsakes to remind you of your visit to this extraordinary city. Take a moment to relax in one of the charming parks or gardens, and let the tranquil ambiance wash over you.

No trip to Bath would be complete without indulging in the city's most renowned offering—the thermal spas. Immerse yourself in the soothing waters of Thermae Bath Spa, Britain's only natural thermal spa. Let the healing properties of the mineral-rich waters melt away your cares and rejuvenate your body and soul.

Whether you're an avid history buff, a culture enthusiast, a food lover, or simply seeking relaxation, Bath has something to offer everyone. This comprehensive guidebook is designed to be your trusted companion as you explore the city's countless wonders. Detailed maps, insider tips, and captivating stories will enhance your journey and ensure you make the most of your time in Bath.

So, embark on this remarkable adventure and let the pages of "A Comprehensive Guide to Bath, England" transport you to a world of timeless beauty and captivating experiences. Discover the city's fascinating history, immerse yourself in its vibrant culture, indulge in its culinary delights, marvel at its stunning architecture, and rejuvenate in its soothing thermal spas. Get ready to fall in love with Bath—the jewel of England.

Safe travels, and may your journey through Bath be as extraordinary as the city.

Annie J Larsen

INTRODUCTION

WHY VISIT BATH?

Welcome to the enchanting city of Bath, a destination that beckons travelers from around the globe with its rich history, vibrant culture, and unparalleled beauty. Nestled in the picturesque county of Somerset, Bath is a place that encapsulates the essence of England's past while offering a vibrant present and a promising future. In this comprehensive guide, I invite you to explore why Bath should be at the top of your travel list.

A Living Tapestry of History:

Bath is a city steeped in history, where each street and building tells a captivating tale. It all begins with the ancient Romans, who discovered the healing powers of the natural thermal springs and established the grand Roman Baths almost two thousand years ago. Immerse yourself in the stories of the past as you walk through the beautifully preserved Roman Baths, where you can witness the remnants of a bygone era and even sample the mineral-rich waters. The magnificence of Bath Abbey, a gothic masterpiece that has stood for over 1,200 years, and the regal elegance of the Royal Crescent and the Circus will transport you to the Georgian era, evoking a sense of grandeur and sophistication.

Architectural Marvels:

Bath's architectural wonders are a sight to behold, showcasing the city's evolution throughout the centuries. Marvel at the masterpieces of Georgian architecture, such as the Royal Crescent and the Circus, which exemplify the symmetry and elegance of the era. The Pulteney Bridge, with its shops and cafes spanning across the River Avon, offers a picturesque view that has captured the imaginations of artists and visitors alike. Explore the stunning Bath Abbey, with its intricate stained glass windows and soaring vaulted ceilings, or venture into the Assembly Rooms, where high society once gathered for balls and gatherings. Each architectural gem in Bath is a testament to the city's rich heritage and impeccable craftsmanship.

Cultural Oasis:

Bath is a vibrant cultural hub that embraces the arts in all forms. The city boasts many museums and galleries, offering a unique perspective on Bath's rich history and artistic legacy. Visit the Holburne Museum in a stunning Georgian building to admire its extensive fine and decorative art collections. The Victoria Art Gallery showcases works by renowned artists, both past and present, while the Museum of Bath at Work provides a glimpse into the city's industrial heritage. For literary enthusiasts, the Jane Austen Centre pays homage to one of England's most beloved authors, inviting visitors to enter the world of Austen's novels and gain insight into her life.

Gastronomic Delights:

Prepare your taste buds for an extraordinary culinary journey in Bath. The city's food scene combines traditional and contemporary flavors, offering diverse dining experiences to suit every palate. Indulge in the delights of a traditional afternoon tea in one of Bath's elegant tea rooms, savoring delicate finger sandwiches, freshly baked scones, and an array of delectable pastries. Immerse yourself in the local cuisine by sampling Bath's famous Sally Lunn bun, a light and fluffy delicacy enjoyed for over 300 years. From cozy pubs serving hearty British classics to award-winning restaurants showcasing innovative gastronomy, Bath will delight even the most discerning food lovers.

Relaxation and Rejuvenation:

Bath is renowned for its rejuvenating thermal spas, offering a blissful escape from the stresses of everyday life. Immerse yourself in the warm, mineral-rich waters at Thermae Bath Spa, Britain's only natural thermal spa, and let the therapeutic properties work their magic on your body and mind. Unwind in the rooftop pool overlooking the city, or indulge in a pampering spa treatment that will leave you feeling utterly relaxed and rejuvenated. The calming ambiance and luxurious amenities of the city's spas create an oasis of tranquility where you can unwind and find serenity.

Natural Beauty and Outdoor Adventures:

Beyond its historical and cultural treasures, Bath is surrounded by breathtaking natural beauty, offering outdoor enthusiasts many opportunities for exploration and adventure. Stroll along the picturesque Kennet and Avon Canal, or embark on a scenic hike through the lush countryside surrounding the city. Discover the enchanting Prior Park Landscape Garden, designed by Capability Brown, with its stunning vistas and tranquil lakes. For those seeking more adrenaline-fueled activities, the nearby Mendip Hills provide a playground for caving, rock climbing, and mountain biking, immersing yourself in the region's rugged beauty.

Festivals and Events:

Bath comes alive with a vibrant calendar of festivals and events throughout the year, ensuring something exciting is always happening in the city. Immerse yourself in the colorful celebrations of the Bath Carnival, where music, dance, and vibrant costumes fill the streets with energy and joy. Explore the literary wonders of the Bath Literature Festival, where renowned authors and thinkers gather to engage in thought-provoking discussions and inspiring readings. The Bath Christmas Market, with its charming chalets and festive atmosphere, is a true winter wonderland, offering a magical experience for visitors of all ages.

Bath, with its rich history, cultural treasures, stunning architecture, and rejuvenating thermal spas, offers an unparalleled experience for travelers seeking a destination that encapsulates the essence of England's past and present. Whether you are captivated by the stories of ancient Romans, enchanted by the elegance of Georgian architecture, eager to explore the city's cultural offerings, or simply looking to relax and indulge in gastronomic delights, Bath has something to offer every visitor. We invite you to embark on a journey of discovery, immersing yourself in the wonders of this captivating city and creating memories that will last a lifetime.

So, why visit Bath? The answer lies in its timeless beauty, vibrant cultural scene, culinary delights, and ability to transport you to a bygone era while embracing the joys of modern living. Let Bath captivate your heart and leave an indelible mark on your soul. Welcome to Bath—where history, culture, and unparalleled beauty converge to create an unforgettable travel experience.

GETTING TO BATH

Bath beckons travelers worldwide with its rich history, stunning architecture, and rejuvenating thermal spas. Whether arriving from a nearby city or embarking on an international adventure, this comprehensive guide will ensure your journey to Bath is seamless and stress-free. From various transportation options to insider tips, we'll guide you to this enchanting destination.

1. By Air:

For international travelers, the closest major airport to Bath is Bristol Airport, located approximately 20 miles away. With excellent transport links, reaching Bath from the airport is convenient and straightforward. Upon arrival, you have several options to choose from:

- Taxi: Taxis are readily available outside the airport terminal, providing a direct and hassle-free journey to Bath. Pre-booking a taxi or using licensed airport taxis is advisable for reliable service.

- Bus: The Bristol Airport Flyer Express bus service operates regular routes between the airport and Bath. This cost-effective option offers comfortable seating and ample luggage space, allowing you to sit back and enjoy the scenic journey.
- Car Rental: If you prefer the freedom of having your transportation, car rental services are available at Bristol Airport. With well-maintained road networks, the drive to Bath is straightforward, allowing you to explore the surrounding areas at your own pace.

2. By Train:

Bath is well-connected to the national rail network, making train travel an efficient and comfortable option for reaching the city. The central train station in Bath is Bath Spa Station, located in the heart of the city center. From London, direct train services to Bath run regularly, with a journey time of approximately 90 minutes. Other major cities, including Bristol, Cardiff, and Birmingham, offer direct train connections to Bath.

When planning your train journey, booking your tickets is advisable to secure the best fares and availability. First Class options are available on many services, offering additional comfort and amenities for those seeking a more luxurious travel experience. Upon arrival at Bath Spa Station, you'll be just a short walk away from the city's main attractions and accommodation options.

3. By Coach or Bus:

Traveling to Bath by coach or bus is cost-effective and environmentally friendly, with numerous services to and from the city. National Express, the largest coach operator in the UK, offers direct connections from major cities across the country, including London, Manchester, and Birmingham.

Bath Bus Station, located centrally, is a hub for local and regional bus services. Regional bus services provide convenient access to Bath if you travel from nearby cities or towns, such as Bristol or Wells. It is worth checking the timetable in advance and allowing flexibility in your schedule, as journey times may vary depending on traffic conditions.

4. By Car:

If you prefer the flexibility of driving, Bath is easily accessible by car via well-maintained road networks. The M4 motorway directly links the city from London and South East England, while the M5 motorway connects Bath to Bristol, the Midlands, and the South West.

Parking in Bath can be challenging, especially in the city center, where space is limited. However, several car parks are available throughout the city, including long-stay options for those planning to explore Bath more. Using Park and Ride facilities on the city's outskirts is advisable, where you can park your car and take a convenient bus service into the city center.

5. Local Transportation:

Once you've arrived in Bath, exploring the city is a breeze, thanks to its compact size and excellent local transportation options. The city center is best explored on foot, as most of Bath's attractions are within walking distance of each other. Strolling through the charming streets allows you to appreciate the city's architecture and ambiance fully.

However, if you prefer alternative means of transportation or need to travel longer distances within Bath, there are additional options available:

- Buses: Bath has a reliable and extensive bus network operated by several local companies. Buses cover various routes within the city and its outskirts, making reaching different neighborhoods and attractions convenient. The bus service offers frequent schedules and affordable fares, and you can obtain tickets directly from the bus driver or through mobile apps.

- Taxis: Taxis are readily available throughout Bath, offering a convenient and flexible mode of transportation. Licensed taxis can be hailed on the street or found at designated taxi ranks. Alternatively, you can book a taxi in advance or use ride-hailing apps for added convenience. Taxis are an excellent option for reaching specific destinations or if you have heavy luggage or mobility requirements.

- Cycling: Bath is a bicycle-friendly city, and cycling is a popular way to get around. The city features dedicated cycling lanes, shared paths, and bicycle parking facilities. If you enjoy cycling, renting a bike allows you to explore Bath at your own pace and discover hidden gems off the beaten path. Several bike rental shops within the city center offer a range of bicycles to suit your needs.

- Walking Tours: Consider joining a guided walking tour to immerse yourself in Bath's history and culture. Led by knowledgeable local guides, these tours offer insightful commentary and take you to iconic landmarks, hidden corners, and lesser-known spots. Walking tours provide a unique opportunity to learn fascinating stories and gain a deeper understanding of the city's heritage.

Getting to Bath is integral to your journey to this enchanting destination. Whether you arrive by air, train, coach, or car, the options are plentiful and cater to various preferences and budgets. Once you've reached Bath, the city's compact size and excellent local transportation system make it easy to explore its attractions, navigate its streets, and uncover its hidden treasures.

As you plan your trip, remember to check for any travel updates, book tickets in advance when possible, and consider the most convenient mode of transportation based on your needs and preferences. Embrace the charm and beauty of Bath as you embark on a seamless journey to this captivating city. With its rich history, stunning architecture, and rejuvenating thermal spas awaiting your arrival, your adventure in Bath will surely be unforgettable.

GETTING AROUND BATH

Once you have arrived in the captivating city of Bath, with its rich history, stunning architecture, and rejuvenating thermal spas, it's time to explore all these enchanting destination offers. With its compact size and excellent transportation options, getting around Bath is a seamless and enjoyable experience. This guide will show you the various modes of transportation available, providing you with the knowledge and tips you need to navigate the city easily.

Walking:

One of the most delightful ways to experience Bath is by exploring its picturesque streets on foot. The city's compact size makes it perfect for strolls, immersing yourself in its charming ambiance and appreciating its architectural treasures up close. Bath's city center is pedestrian-friendly, with many pedestrianized areas and well-preserved historical landmarks within easy reach. As you wander through the Georgian crescents, quaint alleys, and bustling squares, you'll discover hidden gems and experience the city's true essence.

Public Transportation:

Bath benefits from a reliable and efficient public transportation system, offering several options for getting around the city and its surrounding areas.

- Buses: Bath's bus network covers many routes, making reaching different neighborhoods and attractions convenient. Several bus operators serve the city, providing frequent schedules and reliable service. The buses are modern, comfortable, and equipped with accessibility features. For added convenience, you can purchase tickets directly from the bus driver or through mobile apps.
- Park and Ride: Utilizing the Park and Ride service is recommended if you drive into Bath. Park and Ride facilities are located on the city's outskirts and provide convenient parking spaces. From there, you can take a regular bus service that will whisk you to

the city center, avoiding the hassle of city traffic and parking challenges.

Cycling:

Bath's cycling infrastructure and scenic surroundings make it a cyclist's paradise. The city features dedicated cycling lanes, shared paths, and picturesque routes that allow you to explore at your own pace. Renting a bicycle from one of the many bike rental shops in Bath is an excellent way to discover the city's attractions and venture further into the beautiful surrounding countryside. Cycling offers a fun and eco-friendly mode of transportation and allows you to access hidden gems and experience Bath from a unique perspective.

Taxis and Private Hire:

Taxis and private hire vehicles are readily available throughout Bath, providing a convenient and comfortable option, especially for those with heavy luggage or limited mobility.

- Taxis: Licensed taxis can be hailed on the street or found at designated taxi ranks. Bath's taxis are regulated, ensuring professional service and fair pricing. Taxis offer the flexibility of door-to-door transportation, making them a convenient choice for reaching specific destinations or returning to your accommodation late at night.
- Private Hire: Private hire vehicles, and minicabs, can be pre-booked through local taxi companies or ride-hailing apps. This option allows you to arrange transportation in advance, providing peace of mind and ensuring prompt and reliable service.

Sightseeing Tours:

Consider joining a sightseeing tour for a comprehensive and informative exploration of Bath's attractions. These guided tours, led by knowledgeable local guides, offer insightful commentary and take you to the city's most iconic landmarks and hidden gems. From walking to the bus and even boat tours along the River Avon, various options suit your interests and preferred exploration style. Sightseeing tours provide an enriching experience and the convenience of hassle-free transportation and expert guidance.

Accessibility:

Bath strives to be an inclusive and accessible city, catering to the needs of all visitors, including those with mobility challenges. The city offers various accessibility features, such as ramp access to buildings and public transportation, accessible parking spaces, and accessible restrooms. Bath's buses are equipped with low floors, wheelchair ramps, and priority seating, while taxis and private hire vehicles can provide wheelchair-accessible vehicles upon request. Several attractions in Bath, including the Roman Baths and the Fashion Museum, offer accessibility features such as step-free access, audio guides, and tactile exhibits.

Getting around Bath is an enjoyable and straightforward experience, with various transportation options for different preferences and needs. Whether you explore the city on foot, cycle along scenic routes, take public transportation, or join a sightseeing tour, the enchanting city of Bath is waiting to be discovered. With its rich history, stunning architecture, and rejuvenating thermal spas, Bath is a destination that will leave a lasting impression on all who visit. So, pack your comfortable shoes, hop on a bus, or rent a bike, and explore this charming city.

CHAPTER 1: HISTORY OF BATH

ANCIENT HISTORY OF BATH

Bath's stunning Georgian architecture, picturesque landscapes, and rejuvenating thermal spas have captivated visitors for centuries. However, the origins of this enchanting city trace back much further than its Georgian roots. Bath has a rich and fascinating ancient history, dating back over two thousand years. Let us explore the city's ancient past, origins, development, and influence on the modern-day city.

Roman Era:

The history of Bath dates back to the Roman era, when the city was known as Aquae Sulis. The Romans recognized the healing properties of the hot springs and built a complex of bathing facilities, temples, and a grand pump room around the natural hot springs. The complex was dedicated to the goddess Sulis Minerva, a fusion of the Celtic deity Sulis and the Roman goddess Minerva. The

Romans believed that the hot springs had divine healing powers, and people across the empire flocked to Aquae Sulis to bathe in the therapeutic waters.

The Roman Baths complex is now one of the most popular tourist attractions in Bath, allowing visitors to walk in the footsteps of the ancient Romans and experience the grandeur and opulence of the baths. The complex includes the Sacred Spring, the Roman Temple, the Roman Bath House, and the museum, where visitors can view a vast collection of Roman artifacts.

Medieval Era:

After the decline of the Roman Empire, Bath fell into disrepair, and its hot springs were forgotten for centuries. However, the city regained its importance during the medieval era when it became a center for the wool trade and a pilgrimage destination. The medieval city of Bath developed around the hot springs, with narrow, winding streets and timber-framed buildings. The city's religious importance grew with the construction of Bath Abbey, which still dominates the city's skyline today. The abbey's stunning stained glass windows, towering spires, and intricate stonework is a testament to the city's medieval heritage.

Georgian Era:

Bath's most significant growth and development period occurred during the Georgian era, from the early 18th century to the early 19th century. Bath's natural hot springs, scenic location, and peaceful ambiance attracted the wealthy and fashionable Georgian society, who sought to escape the bustle of London and embrace a more refined lifestyle. The Georgian city of Bath is characterized by its elegant crescents, terraces, and squares constructed from honey-colored Bath stone. The most famous Georgian landmarks in Bath include the Royal Crescent, the Circus, and Pulteney Bridge.

Bath also became a center for innovation and technological advancement during this era. The world-renowned architect John Wood the Elder designed many of the city's most iconic buildings. At the same time, his son, John Wood the Younger, continued his legacy and constructed the impressive Royal Crescent.

Victorian Era:

The Victorian era saw Bath's growth and development continue, with the city expanding beyond its historic core. The city's railway station was constructed, connecting Bath to other major cities, and new neighborhoods were developed to accommodate the growing population. The architectural style of the Victorian era in Bath is characterized by its Gothic revival buildings, such as the Guildhall and the Victoria Art Gallery.

As you explore Bath's ancient history, take a moment to reflect on the countless individuals who have walked its streets, from Roman soldiers and Celtic tribes to medieval pilgrims and Georgian aristocrats. Each era has left its mark on the city, contributing to its unique character and architectural splendor.

The preservation and celebration of Bath's ancient history is a testament to the city's commitment to heritage conservation. Through ongoing archaeological excavations, research, and restoration efforts, Bath continues to uncover discoveries and gain insights into its past. These efforts ensure that future generations can continue to explore and appreciate the city's ancient roots.

In addition to its architectural wonders, Bath's ancient history is reflected in its vibrant cultural scene. The city hosts numerous festivals, exhibitions, and events that celebrate its heritage and provide a platform for artists, historians, and performers to showcase their talents. From Roman-themed reenactments to lectures on ancient civilizations, there are ample opportunities to engage with Bath's ancient history dynamically and interactively.

Beyond the tangible remnants of the past, Bath's ancient history has also shaped its intangible heritage. The city's reputation as a spa destination, rooted in the healing powers of the hot springs, can be traced back to the Roman era. The concept of "taking the waters" has endured through the centuries, and today Bath remains renowned for its luxurious thermal spas and wellness retreats, providing visitors with a modern-day connection to the ancient tradition of bathing and rejuvenation.

In conclusion, Bath's ancient history is a captivating tapestry that weaves together the stories of civilizations, the rise and fall of empires, and the evolution of architectural styles. From its Roman origins to its medieval and Georgian periods, the city has evolved and thrived, leaving a legacy that continues to enchant and inspire. As you wander through the streets of Bath, take a moment to reflect on the rich history that surrounds you, and let the ancient echoes guide you on a journey of discovery and wonder.

ROMAN ERA IN BATH

The Roman era in Bath, known as Aquae Sulis, marks an essential chapter in the city's history. During this period, the Romans recognized the healing properties of the natural hot springs and built a magnificent complex around them. The city became a thriving center of Roman civilization, attracting visitors from far and wide to indulge in the therapeutic waters and worship the goddess Sulis Minerva. We shall consider the fascinating details of Bath's Roman era, exploring the grandeur of the Roman Baths, the religious significance of the Temple, and the lasting impact of Roman culture on the city.

The Roman Baths:

The Roman Baths complex is the iconic symbol of Bath's Roman heritage. It is a remarkably preserved site that provides a glimpse into the daily lives of the Romans who once inhabited the area. The complex consists of several key elements:

- The Sacred Spring: The source of the hot springs, the Sacred Spring was believed to be a gift from the gods. The Romans built a reservoir around it, with the water cascading into the Great Bath.

- The Great Bath: The centerpiece of the complex, the Great Bath was a large pool where visitors bathed and socialized. The beautifully constructed walls, adorned with intricate mosaics and statues, reflect the opulence of Roman architecture.

- The Roman Temple: Adjacent to the Great Bath is the Temple dedicated to Sulis Minerva, the goddess associated with the healing waters. The temple served as a place of worship and sacrifice, attracting pilgrims seeking divine blessings.

- The Museum: The Roman Baths complex also houses a museum that showcases a vast collection of Roman artifacts discovered during archaeological excavations. These artifacts, ranging from coins and jewelry to sculptures and everyday objects, provide insight into the daily lives and beliefs of the Romans.

Bath as a Roman City:

Beyond the grandeur of the Roman Baths, Bath was a bustling Roman city with a well-planned layout and impressive architecture. The streets were lined with shops, houses, and public buildings, reflecting the advanced urban planning of the Romans. The city boasted grand villas, temples, and an amphitheater where various forms of entertainment, including gladiator fights and theatrical performances, took place.

The Romans also established a water supply system, with aqueducts and underground channels bringing water from nearby springs to various parts of the city. The remains of these intricate water systems can still be seen today, showcasing the Romans' engineering prowess.

Roman Worship and Beliefs:

Religion played a significant role in Roman life, and Bath was no exception. The Temple dedicated to Sulis Minerva was a focal point of worship, drawing devotees seeking healing, protection, and prosperity. The Romans believed the hot springs were a divine gift and attributed their healing powers to the goddess Sulis Minerva. Visitors would make offerings, prayers, and sacrifices to receive blessings and divine favor.

The Romans also introduced their deities and practices to Bath, blending their religious beliefs with local Celtic traditions. This syncretism resulted in a unique fusion of Roman and Celtic religious practices, further enriching the religious landscape of Bath during the Roman era.

Legacy and Preservation:

The Roman era in Bath left an indelible mark on the city, shaping its identity and cultural heritage. The Roman Baths complex, with its remarkable preservation and ongoing archaeological research, is a testament to the city's enduring Roman legacy. It continues to attract visitors from around the world, who come to experience the therapeutic waters, admire the architectural splendor, and immerse themselves in the ancient atmosphere.

The city's commitment to preserving its Roman heritage extends beyond the Roman Baths. Various Roman artifacts and structures can be found throughout Bath. Excavations have unearthed remnants of Roman villas, townhouses, and mosaic floors, providing valuable insights into the daily lives of the Romans who lived in Bath. These discoveries contribute to the ongoing understanding of Bath's Roman history and allow visitors to appreciate the city's rich cultural tapestry.

Bath's Roman heritage is preserved and interpreted through meticulous conservation efforts and engaging educational initiatives. Skilled conservators work tirelessly to maintain and restore the Roman Baths complex, ensuring its longevity for future generations. The museum within the complex offers immersive exhibits, interactive displays, and informative guided tours, enabling visitors to delve into the past and gain a deeper understanding of Roman life in Bath.

Beyond the Roman Baths, Bath's Roman legacy can be witnessed in its street layout and architecture. The city's grid-like pattern of streets, known as a Roman grid, is still evident in parts of the city center, demonstrating the Romans' meticulous planning and urban design. Additionally, using Bath stone, a local limestone, in constructing buildings throughout the city pays homage to the Roman influence on Bath's architectural landscape.

The Roman era in Bath left physical legacies and impacted the region's economy and trade. The city became a hub for commerce, with merchants and traders flocking to Bath to take advantage of the growing population and the city's reputation as a healing center. The influx of visitors created economic opportunities, supporting a thriving market and the region's prosperity.

Furthermore, Bath's Roman heritage has had a lasting impact on its cultural identity. The city's association with healing and wellness, rooted in the Roman belief in the curative properties of the hot springs, continues to shape Bath's identity as a spa destination. The tradition of "taking the waters" has persisted through the centuries, and modern visitors can experience the same sense of relaxation and rejuvenation enjoyed by their Roman predecessors.

The Roman era in Bath is a testament to the city's rich history and cultural heritage. From the grandeur of the Roman Baths to the meticulously planned city layout, the influence of the Romans can be felt throughout Bath. Their engineering prowess, religious beliefs, and social customs have shaped the city's identity and continue to captivate visitors worldwide.

As you wander through the Roman Baths complex, exploring the Sacred Spring, the Great Bath, and the Temple, you are transported back to an era of opulence, devotion, and communal bathing. The preservation and interpretation of Bath's Roman heritage allow us to understand better the lives of the Romans who once inhabited the city.

Bath's Roman legacy is not confined to the walls of the Roman Baths; it extends throughout the city, manifesting in its street layout, architectural features, and cultural traditions. The Roman era in Bath bridges ancient history and the present, connecting us to a civilization that greatly influenced the city's development.

So, as you visit Bath and immerse yourself in its Roman history, take a moment to appreciate the ingenuity, artistry, and spirituality of the Romans who turned Aquae Sulis into a thriving center of civilization. Their legacy inspires awe and fascination, inviting us to delve into the depths of history and uncover the secrets of the ancient world within the enchanting city of Bath.

GEORGIAN ERA IN BATH

The Georgian era in Bath, from the early 18th century to the early 19th century, marked a period of extraordinary growth and transformation for the city. Bath's Georgian heritage is characterized by its elegant architecture, refined cultural scene, and the influx of the wealthy and fashionable elite. Let's explore the fascinating details of Bath's Georgian era, uncovering the grandeur of the city's iconic landmarks, the social and cultural milieu of the time, and the enduring legacy of this remarkable period.

The Architecture of Bath:

Bath's Georgian architecture is renowned worldwide for its beauty and symmetry. The city's unique use of Bath stone, a golden-hued limestone, lends a warm and timeless charm to the buildings. The Georgian architectural style in Bath is characterized by grand terraces, crescents, and squares, showcasing the principles of Palladianism and Neoclassicism.

One of the most iconic landmarks of Bath's Georgian era is the Royal Crescent. Designed by the architect John Wood the Younger, this curved terrace of townhouses embodies the elegance and grace of the period. Its uniformity, classical proportions, and stunning views across the city make it an architectural masterpiece.

Another notable architectural gem is the Circus, a circular space surrounded by three crescents of townhouses. The Circus represents the collaborative efforts of John Wood the Elder and John Wood the Younger. The Circus is a testament to Bath's Georgian architectural splendor with its beautiful facades, exquisite detailing, and central landscaped area.

Bath as a Social and Cultural Center:

Bath became a vibrant social and cultural center during the Georgian era, attracting the aristocracy, gentry, and artists across England. The city's reputation as a fashionable resort town grew and it was seen as a place for leisure, entertainment, and refined society.

Bath's Assembly Rooms were the heart of the city's social scene. These elegant venues hosted balls, concerts, and gatherings, providing opportunities for the elite to socialize, network, and display their wealth and status. The Grand Pump Room, adjacent to the Roman Baths, served as a meeting place for visitors who came to "take the waters" and enjoy the fashionable ritual of drinking the mineral-rich thermal water.

The cultural life of Bath thrived during the Georgian era, with the establishment of theaters, art galleries, and literary societies. The Theatre Royal, built in 1805, became a prominent venue for theatrical performances, attracting acclaimed actors and playwrights of the time. The city also boasted an active literary scene, with writers and poets finding inspiration in Bath's picturesque landscapes and vibrant atmosphere.

Prominent Personalities of the Georgian Era:

Bath's Georgian era was marked by several influential personalities who impacted the city's cultural and social fabric. One notable figure is Beau Nash, the self-proclaimed "King of Bath." With his wit, charm, and impeccable fashion sense, Nash became the arbiter of taste and etiquette in the city. He shaped the social customs and refined the city's cultural scene, establishing a code of conduct that influenced the behavior of Bath's elite.

Another significant personality of the Georgian era is Jane Austen. Although not a Bath native, Austen spent considerable time in the city and used it as a backdrop for two of her novels, "Northanger Abbey" and "Persuasion." Bath's Georgian elegance and social dynamics served as a rich source of inspiration for Austen, and her works offer a glimpse into the society of the time.

Preservation and Legacy:

The preservation of Bath's Georgian heritage is a high priority for the city, ensuring its architectural treasures and cultural legacy are cherished and protected. The Bath Preservation Trust, established in 1934, has played a crucial role in safeguarding the city's Georgian architecture and promoting its appreciation. Through conservation efforts, restoration projects, and educational initiatives, the Trust has helped maintain the integrity of Bath's Georgian buildings, ensuring that future generations can experience the splendor of this era.

The legacy of the Georgian era in Bath extends beyond its physical architecture. The city's reputation as a cultural and social hub during this time has left an indelible mark on its identity. Bath continues to be celebrated as a center for the arts, with numerous festivals, exhibitions, and events that pay homage to its Georgian heritage. Established in 1948, the Bath Festival showcases music, literature, and the performing arts, attracting artists and audiences worldwide.

Furthermore, the Georgian era's influence on Bath's lifestyle and traditions can still be witnessed today. The city's rich culinary scene, emphasizing fine dining and traditional British cuisine, echoes the refined tastes of the Georgian elite. Elegant tea rooms and historic pubs offer a glimpse into the era's social gatherings and leisurely pursuits. Additionally, the tradition of promenading along the city's grand terraces and crescents continues, allowing visitors to immerse themselves in the same sense of elegance and sophistication experienced by the Georgians.

The Georgian era in Bath represents a golden age of elegance, architectural grandeur, and refined society. The city's iconic landmarks, such as the Royal Crescent and the Circus, stand as testaments to the timeless beauty of Georgian architecture. Bath's vibrant social and cultural scene during this period attracted the elite and continues to captivate visitors with its rich heritage.

As you stroll through the streets of Bath, you will be transported back in time to an era of opulence and sophistication. The architectural splendor, the grand social gatherings, and the artistic endeavors of the Georgian era come alive, immersing you in the spirit of this remarkable period. The preservation of Bath's Georgian heritage ensures that the legacy of this era is cherished and shared with generations to come.

So, as you explore Bath's Georgian treasures, take a moment to appreciate the vision and craftsmanship of the architects, the glamour and refinement of the social elite, and the enduring cultural impact of this era. Bath's Georgian heritage invites you to step into a world of architectural beauty, refined society, and artistic inspiration, offering a captivating journey through time and an unforgettable experience in one of England's most enchanting cities.

MODERN-DAY BATH

As Bath evolved throughout the centuries, it retained its charm and cultural significance. Bath is a modern and thriving city, bustling with life and activity. Despite its modernization, Bath still pays tribute to its history, blending the old with the new to create a unique and vibrant atmosphere.

Culture and Arts:

Bath continues to be a hub for the arts, with a thriving cultural scene celebrating its rich history. The city has numerous museums, galleries, and theaters, showcasing everything from contemporary art to ancient artifacts. The Victoria Art Gallery is a must-visit for art lovers, featuring a stunning collection of paintings, sculptures, and decorative arts. The Holburne Museum offers a fascinating insight into Bath's Georgian era with its exquisite collection of art and artifacts. The Theatre Royal, built in 1805, is one of the UK's oldest and most prestigious theaters, hosting various productions throughout the year.

Bath is also known for its literary heritage, with numerous writers and poets inspired by the city's beauty and history. The Jane Austen Centre, located on Gay Street, celebrates the life and work of the famous author, who spent several years in Bath and set two of her novels here. The annual Bath Literature Festival, held in March, is a popular event that attracts writers, poets, and literary enthusiasts worldwide.

Shopping:

Bath is a shopper's paradise, with a wide variety of boutiques, high-end fashion stores, and specialty shops. The city's famous shopping streets, such as Milsom Street and Walcot Street, offer an eclectic mix of independent retailers and designer boutiques. Bath's markets are also popular, with the Guildhall Market, Green Park Station Market, and Bath Artisan Market offering a range of artisanal products, local produce, and crafts.

Food and Drink:

Bath is renowned for its culinary scene, with a wide range of restaurants, cafes, and eateries offering everything from traditional British fare to international cuisine. The city is particularly famous for its cream teas, served in elegant tea rooms and cafes throughout the city. Bath's pubs are also a popular destination, with many historic establishments offering a range of local beers, ciders, and ales.

Thermal Spas:

Bath's thermal springs have been a significant attraction for centuries, and today the city remains one of the top spa destinations in the UK. The Thermae Bath Spa, located in the heart of the city, offers a range of spa treatments and access to the famous rooftop pool, offering breathtaking views of the city.

Sports and Leisure:

Bath has a vibrant sporting scene, with numerous facilities and activities for visitors and residents. The city is home to

Bath Rugby, one of the top rugby teams in the UK, playing at the historic Recreation Ground. The Bath Half Marathon, held annually in March, is one of the UK's most significant events, attracting thousands of participants worldwide. The city's parks and gardens are also popular destinations for outdoor activities, such as picnics, walks, and sports.

Modern-day Bath is a city that has retained its cultural heritage while embracing modernity. Its rich history, stunning architecture, and thriving cultural scene make it a top destination for visitors worldwide. The city's vibrant shopping and culinary scene and its sporting and leisure facilities offer something for everyone, making it a perfect destination for a city break or a more extended stay.

Whether you're interested in history, culture, shopping, or relaxation, Bath has something to offer. The city's ability to blend the old with the new, the traditional with the modern, makes it a truly unique destination. As you explore the city, take the time to immerse yourself in the modern-day charm of Bath. Start your day with a visit to one of the city's many cafes, where you can enjoy a delicious breakfast while soaking in the vibrant atmosphere. As you walk along the streets, please take note of the modern architectural additions that seamlessly blend with the historic buildings, showcasing Bath's commitment to preserving its heritage while embracing contemporary design.

For those seeking relaxation, visiting the Thermae Bath Spa is a must. Indulge in a spa treatment or unwind in the rooftop pool, surrounded by breathtaking city views. Allow yourself to be transported back in time as you soak in the same thermal waters that have attracted visitors for centuries.

Art enthusiasts will find plenty to admire in Bath's galleries and museums. Explore the diverse exhibitions at the Victoria Art Gallery, featuring works by local and international artists. To taste Bath's Georgian heritage, visiting the Holburne Museum is necessary. Admire the fine art collection and decorative objects that glimpse the city's cultural past.

A visit to Bath would only be complete with sampling the city's culinary delights. From Michelin-starred restaurants to cozy tearooms, Bath offers a range of dining options to suit every taste. Indulge in a traditional afternoon tea with freshly baked scones and clotted cream, or savor a meal at one of the city's renowned farm-to-table establishments, where locally sourced ingredients take center stage.

Sports enthusiasts can catch a game at the historic Recreation Ground, where Bath Rugby competes against top teams across the UK. Join in the excitement as passionate fans cheer on their favorite players and experience the electric atmosphere of a live match.

As the day draws to a close, take a stroll along the picturesque streets of Bath, admiring the twinkling lights that illuminate the city's landmarks. Whether you explore the charming boutiques and artisanal shops or soak in the city's ambiance, the modern-day allure of Bath is sure to captivate you.

Finally, modern-day Bath seamlessly blends its rich history with contemporary flair. The city's cultural offerings, culinary delights, and leisure activities give visitors a rich and engaging experience. Bath's commitment to preserving its heritage while embracing modernity ensures that it remains a captivating destination for travelers seeking a unique and unforgettable experience. So, immerse yourself in the modern-day charm of Bath and discover the perfect blend of old-world joy and contemporary excitement.

CHAPTER 2: CULTURE AND ENTERTAINMENT IN BATH

MUSEUMS AND ART GALLERIES IN BATH

Bath, a city renowned for its rich history and cultural heritage, is home to a vibrant collection of museums and art galleries. These institutions offer a fascinating glimpse into the city's past, present, and future, showcasing diverse art, artifacts, and exhibitions. With this guide, you shall explore the remarkable museums and art galleries in Bath, delving into their unique collections, engaging exhibits, and the cultural tapestry they weave within the city.

The Roman Baths:

Every visit to Bath is complete with a visit to the iconic Roman Baths, one of the best-preserved Roman remains in the world. This ancient site takes you back to when Bath was known as Aquae Sulis, a thriving Roman spa town. The museum at the Roman Baths provides a captivating journey through the history and significance of this ancient site, featuring interactive displays, archaeological finds, and multimedia presentations. Explore the Roman Baths complex, immerse yourself in Roman culture, and learn about the rituals and traditions surrounding using the thermal springs.

The Holburne Museum:

Located in a beautiful Georgian building near the city center, the Holburne Museum houses an exceptional collection of fine and decorative arts. The museum's permanent collection features centuries-old artworks, including Renaissance treasures, 17th-century Dutch paintings, and British portraits. The Holburne Museum also hosts temporary exhibitions showcasing contemporary art and engaging visitors with thought-provoking themes. The museum's elegant setting and stunning collection make it a must-visit for art enthusiasts.

The Victoria Art Gallery:

Situated just a short walk from the Roman Baths, the Victoria Art Gallery offers a diverse range of artworks, from classical to contemporary. The gallery showcases a permanent collection of paintings, sculptures, and decorative arts, including works by artists such as Thomas Gainsborough and Walter Sickert. The Victoria Art Gallery also hosts a dynamic program of temporary exhibitions featuring works by local artists, traveling exhibitions, and thematic displays. With its ever-changing shows and engaging events, the gallery ensures there's always something new to discover.

The Museum of Bath Architecture:

Located in the Countess of Huntingdon's Chapel, the Museum of Bath Architecture provides a fascinating insight into the city's architectural history. The museum traces Bath's architectural evolution from Roman origins to Georgian splendor and beyond. Visitors can explore scale models, drawings, and photographs highlighting the city's iconic landmarks and architectural styles. The Museum of Bath Architecture offers a unique perspective on the city's built environment and its transformation over time.

The American Museum in Britain:

Situated in the picturesque Claverton Manor, the American Museum in Britain is the only museum of Americana outside the United States. The museum showcases a remarkable collection of American folk art, decorative arts, and historical artifacts. Visitors can explore diverse exhibitions highlighting American culture, history, and craftsmanship. The beautiful grounds surrounding the manor provide a serene setting for visitors to enjoy a stroll and the countryside's natural beauty.

The Fashion Museum:

For fashion enthusiasts, the Fashion Museum is a must-visit destination in Bath. Housed within the Assembly Rooms, the museum displays a vast historic and contemporary fashion collection. From elaborate Georgian gowns to iconic designer pieces, the Fashion Museum offers a captivating journey through the evolution of style and fashion. Interactive exhibits, costume displays, and educational programs provide a comprehensive and immersive experience for visitors of all ages.

The Herschel Museum of Astronomy:

Dedicated to the fascinating world of astronomy, the Herschel Museum honors the achievements of the Herschel family, who made significant contributions to the field. Located in the former home of astronomer William Herschel, the museum showcases his telescopes, scientific instruments, and personal belongings. Visitors can explore the family's fascinating history, learn about their groundbreaking discoveries, and even participate in stargazing events and workshops. The Herschel Museum of Astronomy offers a unique perspective on the wonders of the universe and the scientific legacy of Bath.

The Museum of East Asian Art:

Tucked away in a Georgian townhouse, the Museum of East Asian Art offers a captivating journey into the art and culture of East Asia. The museum's collection includes ceramics, jade carvings, paintings, and textiles from China, Japan, Korea, and Southeast Asia. Visitors can immerse themselves in the rich traditions and aesthetic beauty of East Asian art through the museum's carefully curated exhibitions. The Museum of East Asian Art provides a tranquil and enlightening experience, allowing visitors to appreciate the artistry and craftsmanship of this beautiful region.

No. 1 Royal Crescent:

Step into the elegance and grandeur of Georgian life at No. 1 Royal Crescent, a meticulously restored townhouse that offers a glimpse into the luxurious lifestyle of Bath's elite. This museum transports visitors to the 18th century, showcasing period furniture, artwork, and personal possessions that recreate the era's ambiance. Explore the meticulously recreated rooms and learn about the daily lives of the Georgian residents. No. 1 Royal Crescent provides an immersive and authentic experience that brings the past to life.

The Building of Bath Collection:

The Building of Bath Collection is located within the Countess of Huntingdon's Chapel and is dedicated to Bath's architectural heritage. The collection houses architectural models, plans, and artifacts illustrating the city's urban development and achievements. Visitors can delve into the details of Bath's iconic buildings, learn about the city's architectural visionaries, and gain a deeper understanding of the significance of its built environment. The Building of Bath Collection offers a unique perspective on the city's architectural legacy.

Bath's museums and art galleries form a vibrant tapestry of culture, history, and artistic expression. From the ancient wonders of the Roman Baths to the contemporary artworks at the Victoria Art Gallery, each institution offers a unique and enriching experience. Whether captivated by ancient civilizations, intrigued by fine art, or fascinated by architectural heritage, Bath's museums and art galleries have something to offer. Immerse yourself in the captivating stories, exceptional artworks, and immersive exhibits, and discover the cultural treasures that make Bath a genuinely remarkable destination for art and history enthusiasts alike.

THEATRES AND LIVE PERFORMANCES IN BATH

Bath boasts of a vibrant and thriving theatre scene. With its historic venues, diverse performances, and renowned festivals, Bath offers a dynamic platform for live entertainment. In this comprehensive guide, we will explore the fascinating world of theatres and live performances in Bath, highlighting the iconic venues, showcasing the range of performances, and delving into the city's cultural stage.

Theatre Royal Bath:

At the heart of Bath's theatrical landscape stands the illustrious Theatre Royal. This Grade II listed building, dating back to 1805, is one of the UK's oldest and most prestigious theatres. The Theatre Royal hosts many performances, including West End plays, musicals, dance productions, and comedy shows. Its beautifully restored interior and regal atmosphere create an enchanting setting for audiences to immerse themselves in live theatre.

Ustinov Studio:

Adjacent to the Theatre Royal, the Ustinov Studio offers an intimate space for innovative and thought-provoking performances. This cozy studio theatre showcases diverse plays, often featuring emerging talent and experimental productions. From gripping dramas to cutting-edge contemporary works, the Ustinov Studio provides a platform for groundbreaking performances that push the boundaries of traditional theatre.

The Rondo Theatre:

Tucked away in the heart of Larkhall, The Rondo Theatre is a hidden gem that prides itself on promoting local talent and supporting emerging artists. This intimate and versatile venue hosts various performances, including plays, musicals, comedy nights, and cabaret shows. The Rondo Theatre's commitment to community engagement and its inclusive programming make it a vibrant and welcoming space for performers and audiences.

Chapel Arts Centre:

Housed in a converted former chapel, the Chapel Arts Centre offers a unique and atmospheric setting for live performances. This multi-purpose venue hosts an eclectic mix of events, including live music concerts, theatre productions, comedy nights, and art exhibitions. With its intimate ambiance and diverse programming, the Chapel Arts Centre ensures an immersive and memorable experience for visitors seeking cultural enrichment.

Komedia Bath:

Komedia Bath is a lively venue specializing in comedy, music, and club nights. This dynamic entertainment hub hosts a variety of performances, from stand-up comedy shows featuring both established and up-and-coming comedians to live music gigs showcasing local bands and renowned artists. Komedia Bath's energetic atmosphere and commitment to showcasing diverse talent make it a popular destination for those seeking a night of laughter and entertainment.

Bath Festivals:

Bath is renowned for its vibrant festivals celebrating various art forms and cultural experiences. The Bath Festivals, encompassing the Bath Festival and the Bath International Music Festival, are highlights of the city's cultural calendar. These festivals unite world-class performers, musicians, writers, and artists from diverse backgrounds to present a captivating music, literature, spoken word, and visual arts program. The Bath Festivals provide a unique opportunity to immerse oneself in the city's cultural heritage and experience extraordinary performances in breathtaking settings.

Street Theatre and Outdoor Performances:

Bath's streets and open spaces often come alive with the sights and sounds of street theatre and outdoor performances. During the summer, local and international performers take to the city's streets, parks, and squares, captivating audiences with their artistic expressions. Whether it's mesmerizing street performers, lively musical acts, or interactive theatrical experiences, the street theatre and outdoor performances in Bath add an element of surprise and delight to the city's cultural fabric.

Bath's theatres and live performances form a vibrant tapestry of artistic expression, creativity, and entertainment that enlivens the cultural stage of the city. From the historic grandeur of the Royal Bath Theatre to the intimate and experimental productions at the Ustinov Studio and The Rondo Theatre, each venue offers a unique experience for theater enthusiasts. The Chapel Arts Centre and Komedia Bath provide alternative spaces for diverse performances catering to various artistic tastes. Additionally, the Bath Festivals showcase the city's commitment to celebrating the arts on a grand scale, bringing together renowned performers worldwide.

The streets of Bath also serve as a stage for captivating street theatre and outdoor performances, adding an element of surprise and engagement to the city's cultural landscape. Whether it's the mesmerizing skills of street performers, the infectious energy of live music, or the interactive experiences of theatrical installations, the streets of Bath come alive with artistic expression.

Beyond the performances, Bath's theaters and live performances contribute to the city's overall cultural fabric and economic vitality. They provide a platform for local artists to showcase their talent, nurture emerging talent, and engage with the community. The theaters also attract visitors from near and far, boosting tourism and supporting the local economy.

Bath's theaters and live performances offer various experiences catering to different tastes and preferences. Whether you're a fan of classic plays, contemporary dramas, musicals, comedy, or experimental concerts, Bath has something to offer. The city's theaters serve as spaces for entertainment, enlightenment, and escapism, transporting audiences to different worlds and igniting their imaginations.

Attending a live performance in Bath is not just about the show itself; it's an experience that encompasses the city's rich history and cultural heritage. From the moment you step into the grand foyer of the Theatre Royal Bath, with its elegant architecture and sense of anticipation, to the communal laughter and applause reverberating through the intimate spaces of smaller venues, each performance becomes a shared moment that uniquely connects performers and audience members.

Bath's theaters and live performances embody the essence of the arts—the ability to inspire, provoke thought, evoke emotions, and foster a sense of community. They provide a platform for storytelling, self-expression, and celebrating human creativity. Whether you're a lifelong theater enthusiast or looking to explore the world of live performances, Bath's theaters offer an enticing array of options to indulge your artistic sensibilities.

In conclusion, Bath's theaters and live performances contribute significantly to the city's cultural tapestry. From the iconic Theatre Royal Bath to the vibrant street performances, each venue and event offers a different experience that showcases the depth and diversity of the arts in Bath. So, immerse yourself in the magic of live theater, embrace the excitement of cultural festivals, and let Bath's theaters and live performances transport you to new realms of artistic wonder.

FESTIVALS AND EVENTS IN BATH

Bath, a city steeped in history and renowned for its cultural heritage, comes alive with various festivals and events throughout the year. From music and literature to food and art, these celebrations offer a unique opportunity to immerse oneself in the rich tapestry of Bath's cultural scene. This comprehensive guide will explore the exciting festivals and events that grace the city, highlighting their diverse offerings, engaging activities, and the sense of community they foster.

Bath Festival:

The Bath Festival, one of the city's flagship events, takes place annually and celebrates music, literature, and the performing arts. The festival features an impressive lineup of world-class artists, authors, and musicians who grace the stages and venues across the city. The Bath Festival offers a captivating program that appeals to various interests, from classical music concerts to contemporary performances, literary talks, and thought-provoking discussions. The festival's highlight is the Finale Weekend, where outdoor concerts, street performances, and family-friendly activities bring the city alive with a sense of celebration.

Bath International Music Festival:

The Bath International Music Festival is a testament to the city's love for music and rich musical heritage. This festival showcases various musical genres, including classical, jazz, world music, and contemporary compositions. From intimate chamber recitals in historic venues to outdoor concerts in picturesque settings, the Bath International Music Festival offers a unique opportunity to experience the power of music in evoking emotions and creating memorable moments. The festival also incorporates educational programs, workshops, and community events that engage audiences of all ages and backgrounds.

The Great Bath Feast:

For food enthusiasts, the Great Bath Feast is a gastronomic delight celebrating the city's culinary scene. This annual event showcases Bath's diverse flavors, local produce, and culinary talent. From pop-up restaurants and food markets to chef demonstrations and tasting sessions, the Great Bath Feast immerses visitors in a world of delectable treats and gastronomic experiences. The festival also features special events, including food-themed walks, workshops, and masterclasses, providing opportunities to learn about the city's food heritage and indulge in culinary adventures.

Bath Carnival:

Bath Carnival is a vibrant celebration of diversity, creativity, and community spirit. This annual event brings together performers, artists, musicians, and spectators for a colorful and energetic procession through the streets of Bath. The carnival features dazzling costumes, lively music, dance performances, and participatory workshops that encourage people of all ages to join the festivities. Bath Carnival is a joyful celebration that embraces cultural exchange and showcases the city's inclusive and vibrant community.

The Bath Christmas Market:

The Bath Christmas Market is a festive extravaganza that transforms the city into a winter wonderland. This award-winning market brings together over 200 chalets showcasing local crafts, artisanal products, and delicious food and drink. The enchanting atmosphere is enhanced by the twinkling lights, the aroma of mulled wine and freshly baked goods, and the joyful sounds of carol singers. The Bath Christmas Market provides the perfect opportunity to find unique gifts, experience the season's magic, and soak in the festive spirit.

Bath Literature Festival:

The Bath Literature Festival celebrates the written word and the power of storytelling. This event attracts renowned authors, poets, and literary figures who engage audiences through readings, discussions, and workshops. From thought-provoking talks on current affairs to book launches and intimate book club sessions, the Bath Literature Festival offers a platform for intellectual discourse and a deeper understanding of the written word. The festival encourages a love for literature and fosters a connection between authors and readers.

Bath Comedy Festival:

Laughter takes center stage during the Bath Comedy Festival, a hilarious and entertaining event showcasing the best stand-up comedy and comedic performances. With a lineup of talented comedians from national and international circuits, the festival offers side-splitting shows, improv nights, and comedy workshops that leave audiences in stitches. The Bath Comedy Festival brings a dose of humor and laughter to the city, providing a much-needed escape from the stresses of everyday life.

Bath Digital Festival:

The Bath Digital Festival celebrates the city's growing reputation as a digital innovation and creativity hub. This event brings together tech enthusiasts, entrepreneurs, and industry professionals for workshops, presentations, and networking opportunities. From discussions on the latest trends in technology to interactive exhibitions and showcases of digital projects, the Bath Digital Festival highlights the digital landscape's cutting-edge advancements. The festival aims to inspire creativity, foster collaboration, and provide a platform for digital enthusiasts to connect and exchange ideas.

Bath Fringe Festival:

The Bath Fringe Festival celebrates alternative and independent arts, showcasing various performances, exhibitions, and events. From theater and dance to visual arts and street performances, this festival offers a platform for emerging artists, experimental works, and boundary-pushing creative expressions. The Bath Fringe Festival encourages artistic exploration, challenges traditional norms, and invites audiences to engage with innovative and thought-provoking works.

Bath Festivals of Nature:

For nature lovers, the Bath Festivals of Nature is a unique event that celebrates the beauty and importance of the natural world. This festival features talks, workshops, and outdoor activities focusing on environmental conservation, wildlife, and sustainability. From guided nature walks and wildlife photography workshops to informative discussions on conservation efforts, the Bath Festivals of Nature aims to raise awareness and inspire action for a greener and more sustainable future.

Bath's festivals and events create a vibrant tapestry of cultural, artistic, and community experiences. From the Bath Festival and Bath International Music Festival, which celebrate music and the performing arts, to the Great Bath

Feast and Bath Christmas Market, which tantalize the taste buds and evoke the festive spirit, each event offers a unique opportunity to engage with the city's rich cultural heritage. Whether you're drawn to literature, comedy, digital innovation, or the wonders of nature, Bath's festivals provide a platform for exploration, discovery, and celebration.

These festivals entertain, inspire, and foster community and pride in the city's cultural offerings. They bring together locals and visitors, creating opportunities for connection, dialogue, and shared experiences. Bath's festivals and events enrich the city's cultural fabric, contribute to its vibrant atmosphere, and showcase the community's creativity, talent, and diversity.

So, whether you find yourself immersed in the joyous procession of Bath Carnival, captivated by the words of renowned authors at the Bath Literature Festival, or laughing out loud at the Bath Comedy Festival, you'll discover that Bath's festivals and events offer an unforgettable journey through the city's culture, art, and sense of togetherness.

NIGHTLIFE IN BATH

From lively pubs and bars to sophisticated cocktail lounges and late-night entertainment venues, Bath offers various options to suit different tastes and preferences. With this guide, you shall be learning about the captivating nightlife of Bath, highlighting the city's top establishments, popular nightspots, and the unique experiences they offer.

Pub Culture:

Bath's nightlife is deeply intertwined with its traditional pub culture. The city has numerous pubs that exude character and charm, providing a warm and inviting atmosphere for locals and visitors alike. From historic taverns to modern gastropubs, each establishment offers a unique experience. The cozy interiors, crackling fireplaces, and a wide selection of craft beers, ciders, and ales create the perfect ambiance for an evening of socializing and relaxation. Some popular pubs in Bath include The Saracens Head, The Bell Inn, and The Star Inn.

Cocktail Bars:

For those seeking a more sophisticated and elegant experience, Bath has several stylish cocktail bars. These establishments pride themselves on crafting exquisite cocktails using premium spirits, fresh ingredients, and creative flair. With their chic decor and skilled mixologists, cocktail bars like Sub 13, Circo Bar, and The Dark Horse offer a refined and upscale atmosphere. Whether you prefer classic cocktails or innovative concoctions, these venues provide the perfect setting to sip your favorite libations and unwind in style.

Live Music Venues:

Bath's nightlife scene is also enlivened by its live music venues, which showcase various genres and talented musicians. Komedia Bath, a vibrant entertainment hub, hosts live music performances that span multiple genres, including jazz, blues, rock, and indie. The venue's intimate setting creates an immersive experience for music enthusiasts. Moles, another popular venue, attracts local and touring bands, offering an eclectic mix of live music nights and club events. The diverse lineup ensures something for everyone, from avid music lovers to those looking to discover new sounds.

Late-Night Entertainment:

Bath has a selection of late-night entertainment venues that cater to those who want to dance the night away or enjoy a lively atmosphere. Clubs such as Second Bridge and Po Na Na provide energetic spaces for dancing to the latest beats and genres of music. These venues often host themed nights, guest DJs, and live performances, ensuring a dynamic and unforgettable experience. Whether you're a seasoned club-goer or looking for fun and dancing, Bath's late-night entertainment venues have you covered.

Comedy Clubs:

For a night filled with laughter, Bath's comedy clubs offer an entertaining and light-hearted experience. The Komedia Bath Comedy Club showcases a mix of established and up-and-coming comedians, presenting a lineup of side-splitting shows and stand-up performances. The venue's intimate atmosphere creates an immersive experience, allowing audiences to connect with the comedians and enjoy an evening of laughter and entertainment.

Theatrical Experiences:

Bath's vibrant theatrical scene extends into its nightlife, offering unique and immersive experiences for theater enthusiasts. The Natural Theatre Company presents interactive street performances that bring the city's streets and public spaces to life. These unexpected and engaging encounters captivate audiences and provide a different perspective on the city's cultural offerings. Some venues, such as the Ustinov Studio and the Rondo Theatre, host late-night shows and performances catering to night owls seeking a theatrical experience beyond traditional hours.

Wine Bars and Tasting Experiences:

Bath is also home to various wine bars and tasting experiences, perfect for wine connoisseurs and those looking to explore the world of fine wines. The Tasting Room, located in the heart of Bath, offers a curated selection of wine worldwide, allowing visitors to indulge in tasting flights or attend guided wine tastings led by knowledgeable sommeliers. The stylish and relaxed ambiance of wine bars like Le Vignoble and Corkage provides the ideal setting to savor a glass of wine, discover new varietals, and engage in conversations about the nuances of winemaking.

Casino and Gaming:

Bath's casino and gaming establishments provide a lively and exciting nighttime experience for those who enjoy the thrill of games and gambling. The Casino at the Empire offers a range of gaming options, including roulette, blackjack, and poker, accompanied by a selection of bars and restaurants. Visitors can try their luck at the tables or enjoy a drink while soaking in the vibrant atmosphere of the casino.

Nighttime Tours and Ghost Walks:

Bath's intriguing history and supernatural tales come alive during nighttime tours and ghost walks. These guided experiences take participants through the city's hidden corners and mysterious stories. The Mayor's Honorary Guides offer evening walking tours that delve into Bath's history, architecture, and legends, providing a unique perspective on the city's heritage. Alternatively, the Bath Ghost Tours lead visitors through the haunted spots and eerie tales passed down through generations, offering a spine-chilling experience for those brave enough to delve into the supernatural.

Cultural Events and Festivals:

Cultural events and festivals further enrich Bath's nightlife after sunset. The Bath Fringe Festival mentioned earlier, extends its vibrant offerings into the evening, featuring late-night performances, music showcases, and immersive experiences that blur the boundaries between art forms. The Bath Festival also hosts evening concerts and performances, allowing audiences to enjoy live music and theatrical productions under the starry sky. These cultural events provide a unique opportunity to engage with the arts and experience the city's creative energy after dark.

Bath's nightlife scene effortlessly combines elegance, entertainment, and historical charm. From traditional pubs and stylish cocktail bars to live music venues, comedy clubs, and late-night entertainment spots, the city offers diverse experiences to suit every taste and mood. Whether you're looking for a relaxed evening sipping craft beers, a night of laughter and entertainment, or a dance-filled adventure, Bath's nightlife has it all.

Beyond the traditional offerings, Bath's nightlife embraces cultural events, wine tastings, and unique experiences like ghost walks and nighttime tours. These provide opportunities to explore the city's rich history, engage with its vibrant cultural scene, and create lasting memories. So, when the sun sets in Bath, the city comes alive with a blend of sophistication, entertainment, and community spirit, inviting locals and visitors to immerse themselves in the enchanting world of Bath's nightlife.

CHAPTER 3: BATH CUISINES

TRADITIONAL BRITISH FOOD

When it comes to traditional British food, there is a rich tapestry of flavors, influences, and regional specialties to discover. From hearty stews and roasts to comforting pies and classic puddings, British cuisine is deeply rooted in history and reflects the diverse cultural heritage of the United Kingdom. Let us explore the traditional dishes that have stood the test of time, highlighting their origins, ingredients, and the unique flavors that define them.

Full English Breakfast:

Without mentioning the iconic Full English Breakfast, no discussion of traditional British food would be complete. This hearty morning meal typically includes bacon, sausages, eggs, baked beans, grilled tomatoes, mushrooms, and toast. A satisfying combination of savory flavors sets you up for the day. Regional variations may include black pudding, fried bread, or hash browns. The Full English

Breakfast is a beloved institution that embodies the essence of a traditional British start to the day.

Fish and Chips:

Fish and Chips is another quintessentially British dish that has gained worldwide popularity. This simple yet delicious meal consists of deep-fried battered fish, usually cod or haddock, served with crispy golden chips (French fries) and a side of mushy peas. The fish is moist and flaky inside, while the crispy batter adds a satisfying crunch. Fish and Chips are best enjoyed wrapped in newspaper, evoking a sense of nostalgia and seaside traditions.

Roast Beef and Yorkshire Pudding:

Sunday Roast, featuring succulent slices of roast beef, is a cherished tradition in British households. Accompanied by fluffy Yorkshire puddings, roast potatoes, seasonal vegetables, and a rich gravy, this meal is a celebration of family, comfort, and the art of roasting. The Yorkshire pudding, a light and airy pastry made from a simple batter of eggs, flour, and milk, perfectly accompanies the tender beef and flavorful gravy.

Shepherd's Pie:

Shepherd's Pie is a classic British dish that combines minced lamb or beef, cooked with onions, carrots, and peas, topped with creamy mashed potatoes, and baked to perfection. It's a comforting and hearty dish that warms the soul on chilly evenings. Shepherd's Pie originated as a way to use leftover meat, making it an economical and satisfying meal for families.

Cornish Pasty:

Originating from Cornwall, the Cornish Pasty is a handheld pastry filled with meat, vegetables, and seasoning. Traditionally, the filling consists of diced beef, potatoes, onions, and swede (rutabaga) seasoned with salt and pepper. The pastry is crimped along the edge to seal the flavors and create a distinctive shape. Cornish Pasties are a convenient and delicious option for a quick meal on the go.

Afternoon Tea:

Afternoon Tea is a delightful British tradition involving finger sandwiches, scones with clotted cream and jam, and an assortment of sweet pastries and cakes. It's an elegant and leisurely affair with freshly brewed tea, usually enjoyed in the afternoon. Afternoon Tea allows you to indulge in delicate flavors and experience the charm of British tea culture.

Beef Wellington:

Beef Wellington is a show-stopping centerpiece that combines tender beef fillet, savory mushroom duxelles, and rich pâté; all enveloped in buttery puff pastry. The dish is baked until the pastry turns golden and crisp while the beef remains pink and succulent. Beef Wellington is a prime example of British culinary craftsmanship and is often reserved for special occasions and celebratory meals.

Ploughman Lunch:

The Ploughman's Lunch is a traditional British dish that originated as simple meal farmers enjoy in the fields. It typically consists of cheeses, such as cheddar or Stilton, paired with crusty bread, pickles, cold meats, and a hard-boiled egg. The combination of flavors and textures creates a satisfying and well-balanced meal. The Ploughman's Lunch has since become popular in pubs and is often enjoyed alongside a pint of beer.

Bangers and Mash:

Bangers and Mash is a British comfort food dish that combines juicy sausages, usually pork or beef, with creamy mashed potatoes and rich onion gravy. The sausages are often made with a high meat content and seasoned with herbs and spices, providing flavor. This simple yet hearty dish is a favorite among locals and visitors, offering a taste of British home-cooked goodness.

Black Pudding:

Black Pudding, also known as blood sausage, is a traditional British delicacy that may not be to everyone's taste but holds a special place in British cuisine. It is made from pork fat, oats, onions, and blood, giving it a distinct dark color. Black Pudding is often sliced and fried, resulting in a crispy exterior and a soft, flavorful interior. It is commonly served as part of a Full English Breakfast or as a component of a traditional fry-up.

Sticky Toffee Pudding:

For dessert lovers, Sticky Toffee Pudding is a must-try British treat. It is a moist and decadent sponge cake made with dates, covered in a rich toffee sauce, and served with a scoop of vanilla ice cream or a dollop of whipped cream.

Combining sweet, sticky toffee and soft, warm cake creates a heavenly indulgence that will satisfy any sweet tooth.

Trifle:

Trifle is a classic British dessert that layers sponge cake, fruit, custard, jelly (gelatin), and whipped cream. It is a colorful and visually appealing dessert often served on special occasions and holidays. Trifle allows for creativity in flavor combinations and toppings, with variations including sherry-soaked sponge cake, berries, chocolate, or even a splash of alcohol, such as brandy or rum.

Traditional British food celebrates hearty flavors, time-honored recipes, and a sense of nostalgia. From the Full English Breakfast to Fish and Chips, Roast Beef, and Yorkshire Pudding to Shepherd's Pie, each dish tells a story and reflects the cultural heritage of the United Kingdom. Whether you're indulging in a comforting pub meal, experiencing the elegance of Afternoon Tea, or savoring a classic British dessert, traditional British food offers a culinary journey that is both satisfying and memorable. So, embark on a gastronomic adventure and savor the tastes and aromas of traditional British cuisine, where history and flavor come together on a plate.

LOCAL SPECIALTIES

One of the most fascinating aspects of British cuisine is the array of local specialties that vary from region to region. Each area boasts unique flavors, ingredients, and culinary traditions, offering a diverse and exciting gastronomic experience. In this chapter, we will embark on a culinary journey through the different regions of the United Kingdom, discovering the local specialties that make each place genuinely distinct. From the hearty dishes of the north to the seafood delights of the coast, we will delve into the fascinating world of regional British cuisine.

Cornish Pasty (Cornwall):

We begin our exploration in Cornwall, where the Cornish Pasty reigns supreme. Originating from the region's mining communities, this handheld pastry is filled with a savory combination of diced beef, potatoes, onions, and swede (rutabaga). The pastry is crimped along the edge, creating a distinctive shape and sealing the flavors. The Cornish Pasty is a beloved local specialty, perfect for a quick and satisfying meal on the go.

Haggis (Scotland):

When it comes to Scottish cuisine, Haggis is a true icon. Made from a mixture of sheep's heart, liver, and lungs, oats, onions, and spices, Haggis is traditionally encased in a sheep's stomach and simmered to perfection. This hearty and flavorful dish is often served with neeps and tatties (mashed turnips and potatoes) and accompanied by whisky. Haggis is a must-try for those seeking an authentic taste of Scotland.

Welsh Rarebit (Wales):

In Wales, one must catch the classic dish of Welsh Rarebit. Despite its name, Welsh Rarebit is not a rabbit but a delectable cheese-based dish. It consists of a thick sauce made from a blend of melted cheese, butter, ale, mustard, and Worcestershire sauce, which is then spread onto slices of toasted bread and grilled until golden and bubbly. Welsh Rarebit is a comforting and flavorsome treat, best enjoyed with pickles or a crisp salad.

Yorkshire Pudding (Yorkshire):

Moving to Yorkshire, we encounter the beloved Yorkshire Pudding. Although traditionally served as part of a Sunday Roast, these light and airy baked puddings have become popular as a standalone dish. Made from a simple batter of eggs, flour, and milk, Yorkshire Puddings rise to glorious heights in the oven, creating a crisp exterior and a soft, doughy center. They are often served with gravy, making them the perfect accompaniment to a roast beef dinner.

Stottie Cake (North East England):

In the North East of England, the Stottie Cake holds a special place in the hearts of locals. This round, flat bread roll is known for its unique texture and versatility. Its doughy interior and thin crust make it the perfect vessel for filling with various ingredients, such as ham, pease pudding, bacon, or sausage. The Stottie Cake is a satisfying and substantial meal on its own and is a must-try for those exploring the culinary delights of the North East.

Melton Mowbray Pork Pie (Leicestershire):

In Leicestershire, the Melton Mowbray Pork Pie takes center stage. This iconic pie is made with a rich, savory filling of seasoned pork in a golden pastry crust. Its hand-raised construction sets it apart, where the pastry is shaped around a cylindrical mold, resulting in a distinctive bow-sided appearance. The Melton Mowbray Pork Pie is renowned for its superior quality. It is protected by the European Union as a Protected Geographical Indication (PGI), ensuring that only pies made traditionally in the designated area can bear the name.

Scouse (Liverpool):

In the vibrant city of Liverpool, Scouse is a hearty stew that has become a local specialty. This dish is a testament to the city's maritime heritage and cultural diversity. Scouse is a comforting one-pot meal that warms the soul, traditionally made with beef or lamb, onions, carrots, and potatoes. It is often enjoyed with crusty bread or pickled red cabbage. Scouse has deep roots in Liverpool's history and symbolizes its working-class heritage.

Cullen Skink (Scotland):

Heading to the coast of Scotland, we discover the delightful Cullen Skink. This creamy and smoky soup originates from the fishing village of Cullen in the northeast of the country. The main ingredients are smoked haddock, potatoes, onions, and milk. The soup is gently simmered, allowing the flavors to meld together, resulting in a comforting and flavorsome dish. Cullen Skink is a popular choice in Scottish seafood cuisine, offering a taste of the sea in every spoonful.

Eccles Cake (Greater Manchester):

In Greater Manchester, the Eccles Cake is a local specialty that has stood the test of time. This small, round pastry is filled with a sweet mixture of currants, sugar, and spices and wrapped in a buttery, flaky pastry crust. The Eccles Cake is best enjoyed with a cup of tea, allowing the buttery layers to melt in your mouth and the sweet filling to provide a burst of flavor. It is a beloved treat that has become synonymous with the region.

Bath Chaps (Bath):

In the historic city of Bath, Bath Chaps are a unique and flavorsome local specialty. Bath Chaps are made from the cheek and jowl of a pig, which is cured, boiled, and then pressed. The resulting meat is tender and succulent, with a rich flavor. Bath Chaps are often served cold, thinly sliced, and enjoyed with pickles or in sandwiches. They showcase the region's culinary traditions and are a must-try for those seeking a taste of Bath.

The United Kingdom is a treasure trove of regional specialties, each offering a unique culinary experience. These local delights showcase the country's diverse flavors and culinary heritage, from the Cornish Pasty in Cornwall to the Melton Mowbray Pork Pie in Leicestershire and from the Welsh Rarebit in Wales to the Bath Chaps in Bath. Exploring these regional specialties allows you to immerse yourself in the local culture, traditions, and history and truly appreciate the rich tapestry of British cuisine. So, whether traveling through the different regions or exploring the local offerings in your neighborhood, indulge in the delights of regional British cuisine and savor the flavors that make each place unique.

FINE DINING IN BATH

Located in the picturesque countryside of England, Bath is a city renowned for its rich history, stunning architecture, and natural thermal spas. However, it is also a destination that delights food enthusiasts with its exceptional fine dining scene. From charming traditional tearooms to award-winning restaurants, Bath offers diverse culinary experiences that showcase the region's finest ingredients and talented chefs' culinary skills. Join us on a gastronomic adventure as we explore the world of fine dining in Bath, where indulgence and elegance converge.

Bath's Gastronomic Heritage:
To truly appreciate the fine dining scene in Bath, one must understand the city's gastronomic heritage. Bath has a long-standing culinary tradition dating back centuries. With its proximity to fertile farmland and access to fresh local produce, the region has become a hub for gastronomic excellence.

The city's historic Georgian architecture is a backdrop for many exquisite dining establishments. These elegant venues, often housed within beautifully restored buildings, exude charm and sophistication. Bath's fine dining establishments pay homage to the region's culinary heritage, combining traditional recipes and techniques with a modern flair.

Unraveling Culinary Diversity:
Bath's fine dining scene embraces culinary diversity, offering an array of cuisines to cater to every palate. Whether you seek classic French cuisine, contemporary British dishes, or innovative fusion creations, the city's restaurants have something for everyone.

Michelin-starred restaurants, such as The Olive Tree and Menu Gordon Jones, showcase the pinnacle of culinary expertise. With meticulous attention to detail, these establishments present inventive menus highlighting the finest seasonal ingredients. Each plate is a work of art, from delicate seafood dishes to succulent meats and exquisite desserts.

For those seeking a taste of local flavors, Bath offers several venues that celebrate the region's produce. The acclaimed Hudson Steakhouse focuses on locally sourced, dry-aged beef cooked to perfection and served with delectable accompaniments. The Scallop Shell is a seafood lover's paradise, where the freshest catches from the nearby coast are transformed into unforgettable dishes.

The Art of Afternoon Tea:
An exploration of fine dining in Bath would only be complete with experiencing the city's quintessential tradition of afternoon tea. Bath boasts a remarkable selection of tearooms and hotels that offer this indulgent affair in grand style.

The Pump Room, nestled within the historic Roman Baths, is an iconic venue for traditional afternoon tea. Here, guests can relish in the opulent surroundings while savoring delicate finger sandwiches, freshly baked scones with clotted cream and strawberry jam, and an assortment of delectable pastries. The tradition of taking tea at the

Pump Room dates back over 200 years, making it an essential part of Bath's culinary heritage.

Imbibing in Bath's Liquid Delights:
Fine dining in Bath extends beyond exceptional cuisine to include an extensive selection of beverages. The city boasts an array of wine bars, cocktail lounges, and traditional pubs where guests can unwind and savor expertly crafted drinks.

For wine enthusiasts, venues like Le Vignoble offer an extensive wine list featuring local and international selections. Here, patrons can indulge in wine-tasting experiences guided by knowledgeable sommeliers and discover new vintages to suit their preferences.

Cocktail aficionados will find their haven at the Canary Gin Bar, which boasts an impressive collection of over 200 gins. The bar's expert mixologists create exquisite concoctions that showcase the versatility of this beloved spirit.

While exploring Bath's fine dining scene, it's essential to appreciate the art of afternoon tea—a tradition deeply rooted in the city's culture. Indulging in a lavish spread of delicate sandwiches, freshly baked scones, and exquisite pastries accompanied by a pot of perfectly brewed tea is an experience that transports guests to a bygone era of refinement and elegance. Whether enjoyed in the opulent surroundings of the Pump Room or one of the many other tearooms in the city, afternoon tea is an integral part of Bath's culinary tapestry.

To complement the exceptional cuisine, Bath offers a thriving beverage scene. Wine lovers will find themselves spoilt for choice with establishments like Le Vignoble, where they can explore a carefully curated selection of wines worldwide. From crisp whites to robust reds, there's a wine to suit every palate. For those with a taste for spirits, the Canary Gin Bar beckons with its impressive collection of gins and expertly crafted cocktails. Whether a classic martini or an innovative gin-based concoction, the bar's mixologists have perfected the art of mixology.

In conclusion, fine dining in Bath is a journey of culinary discovery that combines exquisite cuisine, elegant settings, and a celebration of the city's gastronomic heritage. With its diverse dining establishments, from Michelin-starred restaurants to charming tearooms, Bath offers an unforgettable experience for food enthusiasts. Whether you're savoring innovative dishes crafted with the finest ingredients or indulging in the timeless tradition of afternoon tea, Bath's fine dining scene promises to leave a lasting impression on your taste buds and memories.

CAFES AND PUBS

In the United Kingdom, cafes and pubs hold a special place in the hearts of locals and visitors alike. These establishments are not just placed to grab a quick bite or a refreshing drink; they are cultural hubs where people come together, socialize, and unwind. Whether you're seeking a cozy spot for a morning coffee, a quaint tea room for afternoon tea, or a lively pub for an evening of camaraderie, the British cafe and pub scene offers a diverse and vibrant experience. Let us check out cafes and pubs in the UK and explore their unique characteristics, historical significance, and the delightful offerings they provide.

1. Cafes: A Haven for Coffee and Conversation

Cafes have become integral to British culture, providing a welcoming atmosphere for coffee enthusiasts and conversation seekers. From trendy artisan coffee shops to traditional tea rooms, restaurants in the UK offer a wide range of experiences.

a) Artisan Coffee Shops:

Artisan coffee shops have gained popularity recently, focusing on specialty coffee expertly brewed by skilled baristas. These establishments source high-quality beans from around the world, carefully roasting and brewing them to create a perfect cup of coffee. Artisan coffee shops often have a laid-back and contemporary ambiance, with minimalist decor and a menu that extends beyond coffee to include a selection of pastries, sandwiches, and brunch options.

b) Traditional Tea Rooms:

For those seeking a more quintessentially British experience, traditional tea rooms offer a glimpse into the country's tea-drinking culture. These charming establishments are known for serving a variety of teas, often accompanied by delicate finger sandwiches, scones with clotted cream and jam, and a tempting array of cakes and pastries. The elegant decor, fine china, and attentive service create an ambiance of refinement and relaxation, making tea rooms famous for indulging in afternoon tea.

2. Pubs: The Heartbeat of British Social Life

Pubs hold a special place in British culture, acting as community hubs where locals and visitors come together to enjoy good company, hearty food, and a wide selection of drinks. Pubs have a rich history and often feature traditional architecture, cozy interiors, and a warm and welcoming atmosphere.

a) Traditional Ale Houses:

Traditional ale houses, often called "locals," are known for their emphasis on real ale and a friendly, unpretentious atmosphere. These establishments serve ales sourced from local breweries, showcasing regional flavors and craftsmanship. A visit to a traditional ale house provides a genuine taste of British pub culture, where you can engage in lively conversation with the locals, play classic pub games, and immerse yourself in the charm of the surroundings.

b) Gastropubs:

Gastropubs have emerged as a popular trend in the UK, combining a pub's convivial atmosphere with a restaurant's culinary delights. These establishments offer an elevated dining experience, focusing on high-quality, locally sourced ingredients prepared with creativity and finesse. Gastropubs often have a menu that ranges from classic pub fares, such as fish and chips or a hearty pie, to more sophisticated dishes that showcase the chef's culinary expertise. With a wide selection of drinks, including craft beers and fine wines, gastropubs cater to food enthusiasts and pub-goers looking for a memorable dining experience.

3. The Pub Culture: More Than Just Drinks

Pubs in the UK go beyond serving drinks; they play a significant role in fostering a sense of community and providing a platform for social interaction. They are gathering places where people come together to relax, celebrate, and share stories. Pubs often host live music performances, pub quizzes, and other forms of entertainment, adding to the vibrant atmosphere.

a) Live Music:

Many pubs feature live music, ranging from local bands and acoustic performances to open mic nights. These musical events create a lively and enjoyable ambiance where patrons can tap their feet to the rhythm, sing along to their favorite songs, or discover new talent. Live music in pubs often spans various genres, including folk, rock, jazz, and blues, catering to diverse musical tastes.

b) Pub Quizzes:

Pub quizzes are a quintessential part of British pub culture. These trivia events bring people together to test their knowledge and compete for prizes. Pub quizzes cover various topics, from general knowledge to niche subjects, ensuring there's something for everyone. Participating in a pub quiz is not only a fun way to spend an evening but also provides an opportunity to engage with the local community and meet new people.

c) Sports Viewing:

Pubs are popular gathering spots for sports enthusiasts, offering a vibrant atmosphere for watching live sporting events. Whether football, rugby, cricket, or any other sport, pubs provide large screens, comfortable seating, and a passionate crowd, creating an immersive experience for fans. Sharing the excitement of a match, cheering for your favorite team, and enjoying a pint with fellow sports enthusiasts is an integral part of the pub culture in the UK.

4. Culinary Offerings: From Traditional Fare to Gourmet Delights

Cafes and pubs in the UK are not just about drinks and socializing; they also offer a wide range of culinary delights, from traditional comfort food to gourmet creations.

a) Traditional Pub Food:

Traditional pub food holds a special place in the hearts of many, with classic dishes such as fish and chips, bangers and mash, and hearty pies gracing the menus. These dishes are often made with locally sourced ingredients and provide a taste of British culinary heritage. Savoring traditional pub food in a cozy and welcoming atmosphere is a cherished experience reflecting British cuisine's comforting and hearty nature.

b) Global Influences:

In addition to traditional fare, cafes, and pubs in the UK embrace global culinary influences, offering a diverse range of dishes to cater to varied tastes. Whether Indian curries, Thai stir-fries, Mediterranean-inspired dishes, or fusion creations, cafes, and pubs provide a culinary journey that transcends borders. Exploring the global flavors allows patrons to indulge in a gastronomic adventure without leaving their local pub.

Cafes and pubs in the United Kingdom are integral to the country's culture and provide a unique and diverse range of experiences. From the cozy ambiance of traditional tea rooms to the lively atmosphere of local ale houses and the culinary delights of gastropubs, these establishments offer much more than just food and drinks. They act as social hubs, where people come together to relax, socialize, and immerse themselves in the vibrant pub culture. Whether seeking a quiet moment over coffee, engaging in lively conversation with locals, or enjoying live music and pub quizzes, cafes and pubs in the UK, provide a warm and welcoming space for people to connect and create lasting memories. So, next time you find yourself in the UK, visit a local cafe or pub and discover the true essence of British hospitality.

CHAPTER 4: STUNNING ARCHITECTURE IN BATH

BATH'S MOST FAMOUS LANDMARKS

Bath is renowned for its rich history, stunning architecture, and cultural significance. Throughout the centuries, Bath has been a place of pilgrimage, a hub of Roman civilization, and a destination for relaxation and rejuvenation. Today, it is home to some of the most famous landmarks in the country, attracting visitors from all over the world. This guide will take you through time and beauty, exploring Bath's most famous landmarks and unraveling their historical and architectural significance.

The Roman Baths:

Every visit to Bath is complete with a trip to the iconic Roman Baths. Built nearly 2,000 years ago, during the Roman occupation of Britain, the baths were a center of social and cultural life. This complex of hot springs and bathing facilities is remarkably well-preserved, offering a glimpse into the opulence and grandeur of Roman civilization. Visitors can walk along the ancient stone pavements, explore the various chambers, and even sample the mineral-rich waters that made the baths famous. The Roman Baths are a UNESCO World Heritage site and provide a fascinating window into Bath's Roman past.

Bath Abbey:

Standing proudly in the city's heart, Bath Abbey is a masterpiece of Gothic architecture and a symbol of religious and spiritual significance. The current abbey dates back to the 12th century, although a place of worship has existed since the 7th century. Bath Abbey is a visual feast for visitors with its striking stained glass windows, intricate stone carvings, and soaring fan vaulting. Stepping inside, one is enveloped in a sense of tranquility and awe. The abbey also offers guided tours, allowing visitors to learn about its history, architectural features, and the religious traditions it represents.

The Royal Crescent:

One of Bath's most iconic landmarks, the Royal Crescent is a row of 30 grand Georgian townhouses that form a crescent shape overlooking Royal Victoria Park. Designed by architect John Wood the Younger in the 18th century, the Royal Crescent is a testament to Georgian elegance and architectural symmetry. The uniformity of the facades, the stately columns, and the ornate detailing make it a sight to behold. Some townhouses are now privately owned, while others have been converted into museums and luxury hotels. A visit to the Royal Crescent offers a glimpse into the city's Georgian past and the lives of the upper classes during that era.

Pulteney Bridge:

Spanning the River Avon, Pulteney Bridge is one of only a few bridges in the world to have shops built across its entire span on both sides. Robert Adam designed this architectural gem in the 18th century, and it is a harmonious blend of functionality and beauty. The bridge features three arches, elegant Palladian-style architecture, and a picturesque weir that adds to its charm. The shops on Pulteney Bridge offer a range of boutique stores, cafes, and galleries, creating a unique shopping experience. Walking across the bridge provides stunning views of the river, the weir, and the historic buildings lining the banks.

The Circus:

Just a short walk from the Royal Crescent, The Circus is another architectural marvel that showcases Bath's Georgian heritage. Designed by John Wood, the Elder, and completed by his son, the circus consists of three curved segments of townhouses, forming a circular shape. The facades are adorned with classical motifs, including columns, friezes, and decorative details. The Circus has a harmonious and grandiose presence, and its circular layout creates a sense of community and unity. Strolling around The Circus transports visitors to a bygone era, evoking the elegance and sophistication of the Georgian Bath.

Sally Lunn's Historic Eating House:

Sally Lunn's is a beloved landmark in Bath and a must-visit for food enthusiasts. Housed in one of the oldest buildings in the city, Sally Lunn's Historic Eating House is famous for its delectable Sally Lunn bun, a light, and fluffy bread-like delicacy. Legend has it that the recipe for these buns dates back to the 17th century when Sally Lunn, a Huguenot refugee, arrived in Bath and brought her unique baking skills. Today, visitors can enjoy a traditional cream tea or a savory dish, accompanied by the famous Sally Lunn bun, in the historical setting of this charming eating house.

The Holburne Museum:

The Holburne Museum is a treasure trove of art and cultural artifacts in a grand Georgian building. The museum houses a diverse collection of paintings, sculptures, decorative arts, and artifacts worldwide. From works by renowned artists such as Gainsborough and Turner to exquisite porcelain and silverware, The Holburne Museum offers a fascinating glimpse into the artistic heritage of Bath and beyond. The museum's stunning gardens, with their beautiful sculptures and tranquil atmosphere, provide a peaceful retreat from the bustle of the city.

Victoria Art Gallery:

For art enthusiasts, visiting the Victoria Art Gallery is a must. Located in a neoclassical building, the gallery showcases an impressive collection of British paintings, including works from the 17th century to the present. The gallery offers a comprehensive overview of British art history, from classical portraits to modern landscapes. It also hosts temporary exhibitions, ensuring there's always something new and exciting to discover. The Victoria Art Gallery provides a cultural oasis in the heart of Bath and is a haven for art lovers.

Bath's most famous landmarks are architectural marvels and windows into the city's rich history, cultural heritage, and artistic legacy. From the ancient Roman Baths to the grandeur of Bath Abbey, the elegant symmetry of the Royal Crescent to the charm of Pulteney Bridge, each landmark tells a story and leaves a lasting impression. Exploring these iconic sites allows visitors to immerse themselves in the beauty and grandeur of Bath while also gaining a deeper understanding of the city's significance throughout the ages. So, whether you're a history enthusiast, an architecture lover, an art connoisseur, or simply seeking to be captivated by the beauty, Bath's famous landmarks will leave you in awe and make your visit an unforgettable experience.

ARCHITECTURAL STYLES IN BATH

Bath in Somerset, England, is renowned for its stunning architecture, which spans centuries and encompasses a wide range of styles. Bath's architectural heritage reflects its rich history, from Roman baths to Georgian splendor. Each architectural style tells a story, blending functionality, aesthetics, and cultural influences. This guide will explore some of the diverse architectural styles found in Bath, highlighting their unique characteristics, historical significance, and enduring appeal.

Roman Architecture:

Bath's architectural journey begins with the Romans, who settled in the area nearly 2,000 years ago. The Roman Baths complex stands as a testament to their architectural prowess. The Roman architects ingeniously designed the baths to harness the natural hot springs, creating an elaborate system of chambers, pools, and steam rooms. Sturdy stone construction, intricate mosaic floors, and grand colonnades showcase the Romans' mastery of engineering and desire to create luxurious and functional spaces. The influence of Roman architecture can still be seen in Bath today, serving as a foundation for the city's architectural evolution.

Georgian Architecture:

From the early 18th to the 19th century, the Georgian era marked a period of elegance and refinement in Bath's architectural history. Bath became a fashionable and prosperous city, attracting high society and leading to a building boom. Georgian architecture in Bath is characterized by its symmetrical facades, classical proportions, and use of Bath stone, a local limestone known for its warm, honey-colored hue. The Royal Crescent, the Circus, and numerous townhouses exemplify the elegance and grandeur of Georgian architecture. These buildings feature decorative elements such as ornate doorways, sash windows, and elaborate cornices, creating a sense of harmony and sophistication.

Victorian Architecture:

The Victorian era, spanning from the mid-19th to the early 20th century, brought about a shift in architectural styles in Bath. Victorian architecture reflects the changing social and technological landscape of the time. Gothic Revival and Italianate styles gained popularity, coexisting with the remnants of Georgian architecture. The Victoria Art Gallery, a neoclassical building, exemplifies the influence of classical architecture during this period. Victorian buildings often feature intricate detailing, such as decorative brickwork, ornamental ironwork, and stained glass windows. The blend of architectural styles in the Victorian Bath adds depth and diversity to the city's architectural tapestry.

Edwardian and Art Deco Architecture:

In the early 20th century, we witnessed the emergence of Edwardian and Art Deco architectural styles in Bath. Edwardian architecture retained some elements of the Victorian era while embracing the simplicity and elegance of the Edwardian period. This style is characterized by its use of red brick, bay windows, and pitched roofs. The Holburne Museum, housed in a former Georgian hotel, exemplifies the Edwardian architectural style in Bath.

Art Deco's bold geometric shapes, streamlined forms, and decorative motifs also marked the city during the early 20th century. The Carr's Hill estate, designed by architect E.J. May for the Stothert & Pitt engineering works, showcases the distinctive features of Art Deco architecture in Bath. These architectural styles demonstrate Bath's ability to adapt to changing design trends while preserving its historic character.

Contemporary Architecture:

Bath's architectural landscape continues to evolve with the addition of contemporary buildings that blend seamlessly with the city's historic fabric. Architects today strive to create structures that complement and enhance Bath's unique setting. The Thermae Bath Spa, a modern thermal spa complex, exemplifies contemporary architecture in

Bath. Its sleek design and use of glass and natural materials harmonize with the surrounding historic buildings, juxtaposing old and new.

Contemporary architects in Bath draw inspiration from the city's architectural heritage while incorporating innovative design elements. Sustainable architecture has also gained prominence, with buildings incorporating energy-efficient features, green roofs, and renewable materials. The SouthGate Bath development, for instance, seamlessly blends modern design with Bath stone facades, creating a harmonious transition from the historic city center to the newer products.

Architectural preservation and restoration also play a crucial role in maintaining Bath's unique character. The Bath Preservation Trust works tirelessly to protect and conserve the city's architectural treasures. Their efforts ensure that historical buildings are maintained, repaired, and restored to their former glory, preserving the city's architectural legacy for future generations.

Bath's architectural styles reflect the city's history and contribute to its cultural identity and tourism appeal. Visitors are drawn to Bath's architectural splendor, immersing themselves in the beauty and heritage of the city. Guided tours and architectural walks allow visitors to explore the diverse styles, learn about the stories behind the buildings, and appreciate the craftsmanship and vision of the architects who shaped Bath's landscape.

Bath's architectural styles form a tapestry of timeless beauty and innovation. From the grandeur of Roman baths to the elegance of Georgian townhouses, the evolution of architectural styles in Bath reflects the city's rich history, cultural influences, and adaptive spirit. Each architectural style adds depth and character to Bath's streetscape, creating a visually captivating and diverse urban environment.

Whether strolling along the grand sweep of the Royal Crescent, marveling at the intricate details of the Roman Baths, or admiring the harmonious blend of old and new in contemporary designs, visitors to Bath are treated to a visual feast of architectural excellence. The preservation and appreciation of these architectural treasures ensure that Bath remains a city of enduring beauty, where the past and present coexist in perfect harmony.

Bath's architectural styles are not merely structures but gateways to the city's history, culture, and artistic heritage. They serve as reminders of the ingenuity and creativity of the architects who have shaped the city over the centuries. As Bath continues to evolve and embrace contemporary design, it remains rooted in its architectural traditions, creating a captivating cityscape that delights and inspires all who visit.

GUIDED WALKING TOURS

Exploring a new city on foot is a delightful and immersive experience. With its rich history, stunning architecture, and charming streets, Bath is the perfect destination for guided walking tours. Led by knowledgeable and passionate guides, these tours offer a unique opportunity to delve into the city's stories, legends, and hidden gems. This chapter will uncover the allure of guided walking tours in Bath, highlighting their benefits, popular routes, and the fascinating sights and landmarks that await eager walkers.

Benefits of Guided Walking Tours:

Insider Knowledge:

One of the most significant advantages of guided walking tours is the opportunity to tap into experienced guides' knowledge. These experts are well-versed in Bath's history, culture, and architectural heritage. They provide fascinating insights, intriguing anecdotes, and lesser-known facts that breathe life into the city's streets. Whether it's the story behind a particular building or the significance of a hidden alley, the guides' expertise enhances the walking tour experience, making it informative and engaging.

Curated Itineraries:

Guided walking tours take the guesswork out of exploring a city. The itineraries are carefully planned to showcase the best of Bath, ensuring that participants take advantage of its iconic landmarks, hidden corners, and local treasures. From the Roman Baths to the Royal Crescent, each stop on tour is thoughtfully selected to provide a comprehensive and well-rounded introduction to the city's highlights. The guides' intimate knowledge of the area allows them to create cohesive and enjoyable routes that maximize the participants' time and provide a seamless experience.

Local Stories and Legends:

Beyond the historical facts, guided walking tours offer a glimpse into the stories, legends, and folklore that make Bath genuinely captivating. Guides share tales of famous residents, significant events, and local customs, breathing life into the city's past. Whether the mysterious hauntings of a historic building or the secrets behind Bath's architectural wonders, these stories add depth and intrigue to the tour, allowing participants to connect with the city more intimately.

Interaction and Engagement:

Guided walking tours foster a sense of community and interaction among participants. As you stroll through the city's streets, you can engage with fellow tour members, exchanging insights, questions, and experiences. The group dynamic adds a social element to the tour, creating a shared exploration that enhances the overall experience. The guides encourage dialogue and are happy to answer questions, creating a friendly and inclusive atmosphere.

Popular Guided Walking Tours in Bath:

Historic City Center Tour:

This tour takes participants through Bath's historic heart, exploring its most iconic landmarks. The highlights are the Roman Baths, Bath Abbey, the Royal Crescent, and the Circus. Guides provide historical context, architectural insights, and anecdotes that bring these sites to life. Participants also have the chance to discover hidden alleys, atmospheric squares, and charming streets that are off the beaten path.

Jane Austen Tour:

Bath holds a special place in the life and works of celebrated author Jane Austen, and this tour takes participants on a literary journey through the city. Guides share fascinating stories about Austen's time in Bath, the places she frequented, and the inspiration behind her novels. From the Assembly Rooms to the Pump Room, participants can enter Austen's world and gain a deeper understanding of her connection to the city.

Haunted Bath Tour:

For those seeking a spine-chilling experience, the Haunted Bath Tour offers a thrilling adventure through the city's haunted past. Guides share spine-tingling tales of ghostly encounters, mysteries, and paranormal occurrences. From haunted pubs to eerie alleyways, participants will explore Bath's dark and mysterious side. This tour provides a unique blend of history, folklore, and the supernatural, making it a memorable and captivating experience for those with a taste for the macabre.

Food and Drink Tour:

Bath's culinary scene is rich and diverse, and the Food and Drink Tour allows participants to savor the city's gastronomic delights. Led by expert guides, this tour takes participants on a culinary journey through Bath's vibrant markets, artisanal shops, and hidden foodie hotspots. Participants can sample local delicacies, learn about traditional recipes, and discover the city's culinary heritage. From the famous Sally Lunn bun to the finest local cheeses and ales, this tour tantalizes the taste buds while providing insights into Bath's culinary culture.

Architectural Gems Tour:

Bath is renowned for its architectural splendor, and this tour focuses on the city's stunning buildings and design. Guides delve into the different architectural styles found in Bath, from Roman and Georgian to Victorian and contemporary. Participants will admire the intricate details of the Royal Crescent, explore the ornate interiors of the Assembly Rooms, and learn about the city's architectural preservation efforts. This tour celebrates Bath's architectural heritage, showcasing design evolution throughout the centuries.

Tips on how to enjoy your Guided Walking Tours:

- Dress comfortably: Wear comfortable shoes and dress appropriately for the weather. Bath is known for its cobbled streets, so comfortable footwear is essential for an enjoyable walking tour.

- Bring a water bottle: Staying hydrated is essential, especially during more extended tours. Carry a water bottle to keep you refreshed throughout the walk.

- Be prepared for weather changes: Bath's weather can be unpredictable, so it's a good idea to bring a light rain jacket or umbrella in case of sudden showers.

- Ask questions: Guides are a wealth of knowledge, so don't hesitate to ask questions and engage in conversation. They are there to enhance your experience and share their passion for the city.

- Take your time: Walking tours are meant to be enjoyed leisurely, allowing participants to take in the sights, capture photographs, and soak up the atmosphere. Don't rush and savor every moment.

Guided walking tours offer a captivating and immersive way to discover the enchanting city of Bath. With knowledgeable guides, curated itineraries, and engaging narratives, these tours provide a deeper understanding of the city's history, culture, and architectural marvels. Whether you explore Bath's historic landmarks, delve into its literary connections, or embark on a culinary adventure, each guided walking tour offers a unique perspective and an unforgettable experience. So lace up your walking shoes, join a guided tour, and let the enchantment of Bath unfold step by step.

CHAPTER 5: RELAXING THERMAL SPAS IN BATH

HISTORY OF BATH'S THERMAL SPAS

Bath has been renowned for its thermal spas for centuries. Its natural hot springs' healing properties have attracted visitors worldwide, making it a hub of wellness and relaxation. Steeped in rich history, Bath's thermal spas have witnessed empires' rise and fall, societies' rejuvenation, and the evolution of architectural marvels. Join me on a captivating journey as we delve into the history of Bath's thermal spas, exploring their origins, significance, and enduring legacy.

Ancient Origins and Roman Influence:

The story of Bath's thermal spas begins over two thousand years ago during the Roman occupation of Britain. The Romans, renowned for their appreciation of bathing and its therapeutic benefits, were captivated by the hot springs they discovered in Bath. They built a magnificent complex known as Aquae Sulis, dedicated to the goddess Sulis Minerva, transforming the area into a thriving center of relaxation and healing.

The Roman Baths, the centerpiece of Aquae Sulis, showcased the architectural prowess of the time. The complex featured a series of bathing chambers, a sacred temple, and an ingenious plumbing system allowing natural hot spring water flow. The Romans believed the mineral-rich waters possessed curative properties, curing various ailments and promoting well-being.

Decline and Revival:

With the decline of the Roman Empire, the once-grand thermal spas of Bath fell into disrepair. The knowledge of their healing properties gradually faded into obscurity, and the baths became forgotten relics of a bygone era. However, their significance was revived during the 18th century, known as the Georgian era, when Bath experienced a resurgence as a fashionable and elegant city.

The revival of Bath's thermal spas can be attributed to the efforts of individuals such as Ralph Allen and John Wood the Elder, who recognized the potential of the city's natural hot springs. They spearheaded the development of Bath's grand architecture, including constructing the iconic Pump Room and the stunning Royal Crescent. This rejuvenation included the restoration of the Roman Baths and the establishment of new spa facilities.

The Georgian Era and Bath's Golden Age:

The Georgian era marked Bath's golden age, and the city's thermal spas were central to its prosperity. Bath became a fashionable destination for the British aristocracy, who flocked to the city seeking leisure and treatment. The elegant Georgian buildings and refined social gatherings created a sophisticated ambiance that attracted notable figures such as Jane Austen and Beau Nash.

Bath's thermal spas evolved into opulent establishments catering to the wealthy elite during this period. The Pump Room, with its grand interiors and live music, became the social epicenter where visitors would gather to see and be seen. Here, guests would indulge in the tradition of taking the healing waters, believed to alleviate various ailments, from rheumatism to gout.

Victorian Era and Innovations:
The Victorian era brought further advancements to Bath's thermal spas. With new technologies and a growing interest in scientific discoveries, the spas embraced innovative treatments and expanded their facilities. The construction of the Grand Pump Room Hotel and the Thermae Bath Spa showcased the city's commitment to providing a luxurious and immersive spa experience.

The Thermae Bath Spa opened in 2006 and was a modern marvel combining ancient and contemporary elements. It offered a state-of-the-art rooftop pool with panoramic views, where visitors could immerse themselves in the mineral-rich waters while enjoying the cityscape. The spa also incorporated various treatments and therapies, including massages, steam rooms, and aromatherapy, providing a holistic approach to well-being.

Preservation and UNESCO World Heritage Status:
Recognizing Bath's thermal spas' historical and cultural significance, the city was designated as a UNESCO World Heritage Site in 1987. This prestigious status acknowledges Bath's exceptional universal value, including its thermal spas, architectural marvels, and unique blend of Roman and Georgian influences.

Preservation efforts have been paramount in maintaining the integrity of Bath's thermal spas. The Roman Baths, meticulously restored and enhanced with informative exhibits, remain a significant tourist attraction. Visitors can explore the ancient bathing chambers, walk on the original Roman pavement, and even taste the mineral-rich waters from the King's Bath.

In addition to the Roman Baths, the Thermae Bath Spa exemplifies the city's commitment to preserving and celebrating its thermal spa heritage. The modern spa complex seamlessly integrates with the historic architecture, offering a contemporary wellness experience while respecting the city's historical context.

Legacy and Modern-day Experience:

The legacy of Bath's thermal spas is a testament to the enduring allure of healing waters. Today, visitors to Bath can immerse themselves in a range of spa experiences that combine tradition, innovation, and relaxation. Whether indulging in a luxurious spa treatment, soaking in the warm mineral-rich waters, or simply through the beautifully preserved Georgian streets, Bath's thermal spas continue to captivate and rejuvenate.

Moreover, Bath's thermal spas have become an integral part of the city's identity, shaping its tourism industry and providing a unique cultural experience for visitors. The combination of history, architecture, and wellness creates a harmonious blend that sets Bath apart as a sought-after destination for those seeking relaxation, cultural enrichment, and a connection to the past.

Bath's thermal spas have a captivating history that stretches back thousands of years, from their origins as a Roman center of bathing and healing to their revival during the Georgian era. These natural hot springs have witnessed the rise and fall of civilizations, the transformation of architectural landscapes, and the continuous pursuit of well-being. Today, Bath's thermal spas stand as remarkable testaments to the enduring power of water, attracting visitors from around the world to immerse themselves in a blend of history, relaxation, and rejuvenation.

BATH'S TOP SPAS AND THERMAL BATHS

With a history dating back to Roman times, Bath has long been celebrated for its natural hot springs and therapeutic properties. Some of Bath's top spas and thermal baths, their unique features, healing traditions, and the ultimate pampering experiences they offer are:

Thermae Bath Spa:

No visit to Bath is complete without a trip to the iconic Thermae Bath Spa. This award-winning spa is the only place in the UK where you can bathe in natural thermal waters. The star attraction is the open-air rooftop pool, where you can immerse yourself in the warm, mineral-rich waters while enjoying breathtaking views of the city's skyline. Indulge in the spa's luxurious treatments, including massages, facials, and body wraps, to enhance your well-being and relaxation.

The Gainsborough Bath Spa:

Situated within a historic building, The Gainsborough Bath Spa offers a truly luxurious and immersive experience. Drawing water from the city's thermal springs, the spa boasts a range of exquisite thermal pools, each with different temperatures and healing properties. The spa's beautiful decor and attention to detail enhance the unique floating experience in the warm, mineral-rich waters. The Gainsborough also offers various treatments, including tailored massages and signature rituals that combine ancient techniques with modern wellness practices.

Roman Baths:

For a truly immersive journey into Bath's rich history, a visit to the Roman Baths is a must. These ancient bathing and socializing complexes were built around the city's natural hot springs over 2,000 years ago. While the Roman Baths no longer offer bathing facilities, visitors can explore the remarkable ruins, including the Great Bath, the Sacred Spring, and the Roman Temple. The interactive museum provides fascinating insights into the Roman bathing rituals and the significance of the thermal waters.

Cross Bath:

Tucked away in a secluded courtyard, the Cross Bath is a hidden gem that offers an intimate and serene spa experience. This open-air thermal bath, surrounded by ancient stone walls, provides a tranquil setting to unwind and soak in the therapeutic waters. The Cross Bath is available for private hire, allowing guests to enjoy an exclusive and personalized experience. Immerse yourself in the warm waters, surrounded by history and tranquility.

Spa 15:

For those seeking a unique blend of relaxation and culinary delights, Spa 15 is the perfect choice. Located within No.15 Great Pulteney, a boutique hotel in Bath, this spa offers a range of indulgent treatments combined with a Champagne and cocktail bar. Unwind with a luxurious massage or facial, and savor a selection of expertly crafted cocktails or a glass of Champagne. Spa 15 provides a vibrant and sophisticated environment where pampering meets gastronomic pleasure.

Bath Spa Hotel:

Perched on a hillside overlooking the city, Bath Spa Hotel combines breathtaking views with a tranquil spa experience. The spa offers a range of treatments and therapies, including traditional massages, holistic rituals, and beauty treatments. The highlight is the heated outdoor swimming pool, where you can relax while admiring panoramic vistas of Bath's skyline. The serene setting and the spa's professional staff ensure a peaceful and rejuvenating experience.

The Royal Crescent Hotel & Spa:

Immerse yourself in luxury at The Royal Crescent Hotel & Spa, an iconic landmark in Bath. The spa at this prestigious hotel offers a serene oasis, complete with an indoor pool, sauna, and steam room. Indulge in a wide range of spa treatments, from soothing massages to rejuvenating facials tailored to your needs. The elegant surroundings and impeccable service at The Royal Crescent Hotel & Spa create a rich and indulgent experience.

Combe Grove:

Escape the hustle and bustle of the city at Combe Grove, a country club and spa nestled in 70 acres of picturesque parkland. The spa offers a range of treatments using organic and natural products, promoting holistic wellness and relaxation. Unwind in the heated indoor pool, take a rejuvenating dip in the outdoor hot tub, or pamper yourself with a luxurious spa ritual. Combe Grove's tranquil setting and emphasis on well-being make it a perfect retreat for those seeking peace and serenity.

The Bath Priory Hotel:

Experience luxury and tranquility at The Bath Priory Hotel's spa. Set within beautiful gardens, this intimate spa offers a variety of treatments that blend modern techniques with traditional therapies. From massages to facials, each treatment is designed to restore balance and promote a sense of well-being. After your spa session, relax in the peaceful garden or enjoy a refreshing drink at the spa lounge, soaking in the serenity of the surroundings.

Homewood:

Escape to Homewood, a boutique hotel and spa just a short drive from Bath city center. This contemporary spa offers a range of luxurious treatments, including massages, body wraps, and facials, all aimed at revitalizing the body and mind. Relax in the indoor hydrotherapy pool or detoxify in the sauna and steam room. Homewood's serene atmosphere and personalized approach ensure a truly rejuvenating experience.

Tips for a Spa and Thermal Bath Visits:

1. Book in advance: Spa and thermal bath experiences are popular, so booking your treatments or sessions is advisable to secure your preferred time slot.

2. Arrive early: Arriving early lets you maximize the spa facilities and ensure a relaxed and unhurried experience. Enjoy the sauna, steam room, or relaxation areas before your treatment.

3. Communicate your preferences: When booking treatments, communicate your preferences and any specific concerns or allergies to the spa staff. This ensures they can tailor the experience to your needs and provide a truly personalized service.

4. Stay hydrated: Drinking water before and after your spa or thermal bath experience is essential to stay hydrated and maximize the benefits of the treatments.

5. Relax and disconnect: Embrace the opportunity to disconnect from the outside world and immerse yourself in relaxation. Switch off your phone and unwind and enjoy the tranquil environment fully.

Bath's top spas and thermal baths offer relaxation and rejuvenation, where you can immerse yourself in the city's rich history and natural healing properties. Whether you choose to soak in the thermal waters, indulge in luxurious spa treatments, or unwind in the serene surroundings, these experiences provide a blissful escape from the stresses of everyday life. With their unique features, professional staff, and commitment to well-being, Bath's spas and thermal baths promise a genuinely indulgent and revitalizing experience for visitors seeking the ultimate pampering retreat.

CHOOSING THE RIGHT SPA EXPERIENCE

In our fast-paced and stressful lives, self-care and relaxation are essential. A spa experience offers the perfect opportunity to unwind, rejuvenate, and pamper yourself. However, choosing the right spa experience can be overwhelming with many options. This guide will help you explore the key factors to consider when selecting a spa, ensuring you find the perfect retreat tailored to your needs and preferences.

Determine Your Goals:

Before embarking on your spa journey, defining your goals is essential. What do you hope to achieve from your spa experience? Are you looking to relax, de-stress, revitalize your body and mind, or address specific health concerns? Identifying your goals will help narrow your options and ensure you choose a spa that aligns with your desired outcomes.

Consider the Spa Type:

Spas come in various forms, each offering a unique experience. Some common spa types include:

- Resort Spas: These spas are often located within luxury resorts and offer comprehensive treatments and facilities. They are ideal for those seeking a full wellness retreat, with options for accommodation, fitness activities, and gourmet dining.

- Day Spas: Day spas provide a shorter-term escape, usually without overnight accommodation. They offer a variety of treatments, ranging from massages and facials to body wraps and beauty services. Day spas are perfect for those seeking a quick relaxation or a special treat.

- Medical Spas: Medical spas combine traditional spa treatments with medical procedures, such as Botox, laser treatments, and cosmetic surgeries. They are ideal for individuals seeking both aesthetic enhancements and therapeutic benefits under the supervision of medical professionals.

- Wellness Retreats: Wellness retreats focus on holistic well-being, encompassing physical, mental, and spiritual aspects. They often include yoga, meditation, healthy cuisine, and personalized wellness programs. Wellness retreats are perfect for those seeking a comprehensive wellness experience.

Consider which spa type resonates with your preferences and aligns with your desired experience.

Assess Spa Facilities and Amenities:

The facilities and amenities of a spa play a crucial role in enhancing your overall experience. Some aspects to consider include:

- Treatment Rooms: Check if the spa has well-appointed treatment rooms that create a serene and comfortable ambiance. Look for features like heated beds, soothing music, and soft lighting to ensure a tranquil treatment setting.

- Relaxation Areas: A good spa should provide relaxation areas to unwind before or after your treatments. Look for amenities like cozy lounges, quiet rooms, outdoor spaces, or meditation areas where you can relax and soak in the serenity of the surroundings.

- Hydrotherapy Facilities: Hydrotherapy facilities, such as saunas, steam rooms, whirlpools, or hydrotherapy pools, offer additional therapeutic benefits. These amenities can help soothe muscles, improve circulation, and promote relaxation.

- Fitness and Wellness Facilities: If maintaining an active lifestyle is essential, consider spas that offer fitness centers, yoga studios, or wellness classes. These facilities provide opportunities to engage in physical activities that complement your spa experience.

- Additional Amenities: Some spas may offer extra amenities like swimming pools, hot tubs, beauty salons, or gourmet restaurants. Assess whether these amenities align with your preferences and contribute to your desired spa experience.

Research Spa Treatments and Services:

The spa's range of treatments and services is crucial in choosing the right experience. Research the spa's menu and explore the types of treatments available. Consider whether you prefer traditional massages, facials, body treatments, or specialized therapies such as Ayurvedic or energy healing modalities. Look for spas that offer treatments tailored to your specific needs or concerns, such as deep tissue massages for muscle tension or anti-aging facials for skin care.

Additionally, consider the qualifications and expertise of the spa's therapists and practitioners. Look for spas that employ trained professionals with experience in delivering high-quality treatments. Check for any certifications or accreditations that ensure the therapists meet industry standards.

Read Reviews and Seek Recommendations:

Before making a final decision, take the time to read reviews and seek recommendations from trusted sources. Online review platforms, travel websites, and social media platforms are valuable resources for gathering feedback from previous spa guests. Pay attention to both positive and negative reviews to get a well-rounded understanding of the spa's strengths and weaknesses.

Seek recommendations from friends, family, or colleagues who have had positive spa experiences. Personal referrals can provide valuable insights and help you make an informed decision.

Consider Location and Accessibility:

Consider the location and accessibility of the spa, especially if you're planning a day spa visit or a short getaway. If you're seeking relaxation, choose a spa in a peaceful and picturesque setting, away from the noise and chaos of urban life. On the other hand, if you prefer convenience, opt for a spa that is easily accessible and located in proximity to your accommodation or transportation hubs.

Budget and Value for Money:

Spa experiences can vary significantly in terms of cost. Before finalizing your choice, consider your budget and assess the value for money offered by the spa. Consider the quality of treatments, facilities, and overall experience at a price. Some spas may offer package deals or seasonal promotions that provide excellent value for money.

Personal Preferences and Atmosphere:

Lastly, trust your instincts and consider your personal preferences. Think about the atmosphere and ambiance that appeals to you. Do you prefer a tranquil, minimalist spa setting or a more opulent and luxurious environment? Consider whether the spa's overall vibe aligns with your tastes and preferences.

Choosing the right spa experience is a personal journey that requires careful consideration of your different spas' goals, preferences, and offerings. By determining your goals, considering the spa type, assessing facilities and amenities, researching treatments and services, reading reviews, and viewing location, accessibility, budget, and personal preferences, you can make an informed decision.

Remember, the perfect spa experience aligns with your desires and provides relaxation and rejuvenation. So, take the time to choose wisely and embark on a spa journey that will leave you feeling pampered, refreshed, and revitalized.

SPA ETIQUETTE AND TIPS

Visiting a spa is a beautiful opportunity to relax, rejuvenate, and care for your well-being. Proper spa etiquette ensures a pleasant and stress-free experience for yourself and others. Let me give you some spa etiquette guidelines and helpful tips to enhance your spa visit and maximize your time in this tranquil oasis.

Arrival and Check-In:

Arriving on time is crucial to fully enjoy your spa experience and allow a smooth transition between treatments. Aim to arrive at least 15 minutes before your appointment to check in, complete the necessary paperwork, and prepare for your treatments. Arriving early also gives you time to unwind and familiarize yourself with the spa facilities.

Communication and Preferences:

Effective communication with the spa staff is critical to ensuring your comfort and satisfaction. When booking your appointment, inform the staff about any specific concerns, allergies, or preferences you may have. This will help them tailor the treatments to your needs and provide a personalized experience.

During your consultation with the therapist, communicate your preferences regarding pressure, temperature, and any areas of focus or sensitivity. Feel free to ask questions or provide feedback throughout the treatment to ensure your comfort and maximize the benefits.

Dress Code and Attire:

Spas usually provide robes, towels, and slippers for your convenience. Follow the spa's dress code guidelines, including wearing swimwear for specific treatments or utilizing disposable undergarments. Remember that the spa is a place of relaxation and modesty, so respecting the comfort and privacy of other guests is essential.

Mobile Phones and Electronics:

To maintain a tranquil atmosphere and allow everyone to unwind fully, it's best to switch off your mobile phone or set it to silent mode before entering the spa. The spa environment should be a relaxing sanctuary, so avoid using electronic devices in common areas or treatment rooms. Embrace the opportunity to disconnect from the digital world and focus on your well-being.

Hygiene and Health Considerations:

Maintaining proper hygiene is essential in a spa setting. Before your treatment, shower to ensure cleanliness and remove oils or lotions from your skin. Avoid wearing heavy perfumes or fragrances that may interfere with the spa experience of other guests.

If you have health concerns or medical conditions, inform the spa staff during the booking process. They can guide suitable treatments and ensure your safety and well-being.

Respectful Behavior:

Spas are serene spaces where guests come to relax and unwind. To maintain a peaceful atmosphere, it's essential to be mindful of your behavior and respect the privacy of other guests. Keep conversations quiet and avoid disruptive activities, such as loud music or excessive use of personal devices.

Tipping and Gratuity:

Tipping is a common practice in the spa industry to show appreciation for excellent service. While tipping policies may vary, a general guideline is to leave a gratuity of 15-20% of the total treatment cost. Some spas include the prize in the final bill, while others allow you to leave a cash tip for the therapist. Ask the front desk for guidance if you need clarification about the spa's tipping policy.

Post-Treatment Relaxation:

After your treatment, take some time to relax and enjoy the spa's facilities. Many spas offer relaxation areas, steam rooms, saunas, or lounges where you can unwind and savor the post-treatment tranquility. Allow yourself to fully embrace the treatment's benefits before returning to your daily routine.

Maintaining a Quiet Environment:

Spas aim to provide a peaceful environment for guests to unwind. Maintaining a quiet environment is essential to contribute to this serene atmosphere. Keep your voice low when conversing with others and avoid loud or disruptive behavior. Respect the tranquility of the space by refraining from using mobile phones or engaging in noisy activities.

Spa Facilities and Equipment:

Respect the spa's facilities and equipment by using them as intended and handling them carefully. This includes gym equipment, sauna and steam room controls, hot tubs, and other amenities. Follow spa staff guidelines and leave the facilities clean and tidy for the next guest to enjoy.

Spa Etiquette for Couples or Groups:

If you're visiting the spa with a partner or a group, it's essential to be considerate of other guests. Keep conversations at a low volume and avoid any excessive displays of affection or disruptive behavior. Maintain a respectful and peaceful atmosphere to ensure all guests can enjoy their spa experience.

Relaxation and Mindfulness:

Embrace the spirit of relaxation and mindfulness during your spa visit. Take the opportunity to disconnect from daily stressors and focus on your well-being. Engage in deep breathing exercises, meditation, or be fully present. Use the spa experience to nurture your mind, body, and soul.

Follow Spa Policies and Rules:

Every spa has its own set of policies and rules designed to ensure the safety and comfort of all guests. Familiarize yourself with these guidelines and adhere to them during your visit. This may include procedures related to swimwear, use of facilities, or restrictions on specific treatments. Following the spa's policies contributes to a pleasant experience for everyone.

Post-Spa Care:

After your spa visit, continue to nurture your well-being by practicing self-care at home. Drink plenty of water to stay hydrated, especially if you've enjoyed treatments like massages or body wraps. Avoid vigorous activities or exposure to extreme temperatures immediately after your visit to allow your body to benefit from the relaxation and rejuvenation fully.

Following proper spa etiquette enhances your experience and that of other guests. From arriving on time to respecting the tranquility of the space, these guidelines ensure a pleasant spa visit. Remember to communicate your preferences, practice mindfulness, and embrace the opportunity for self-care and relaxation. Doing so maximizes your spa experience's benefits and leaves you feeling rejuvenated, refreshed, and ready to face the world with a renewed sense of well-being.

CHAPTER 6: ACCOMMODATIONS IN BATH

LUXURY HOTELS IN BATH

With its rich history, stunning architecture, and picturesque charm, Bath is an ideal destination for a luxurious and memorable getaway. As you explore the city's fascinating attractions and immerse yourself in its cultural heritage, staying at a luxury hotel will elevate your experience to new heights of opulence and comfort. Check out the world of luxury hotels in Bath, their unique features, exceptional services, and the unrivaled experiences they offer to discerning travelers.

The Gainsborough Bath Spa:

Situated in the heart of Bath, The Gainsborough Bath Spa is a haven of luxury and relaxation. Housed within a historic building, this five-star hotel seamlessly blends traditional elegance with contemporary style. The pièce de résistance of this hotel is its thermal spa, which draws its water from Bath's natural thermal springs. Guests can indulge in rejuvenating spa treatments and soak in the healing waters, immersing themselves in the city's ancient wellness traditions. The Gainsborough also boasts exquisitely appointed rooms and suites, personalized service, and a Michelin-starred restaurant that offers a culinary journey of the senses.

The Royal Crescent Hotel & Spa:

Nestled within Bath's iconic Royal Crescent, this five-star hotel is an architectural gem that offers a truly refined experience. The Royal Crescent Hotel & Spa showcases Georgian grandeur at its finest, with elegantly furnished rooms, lavish suites, and impeccable service. The hotel's spa is a sanctuary of tranquility, offering a range of luxurious treatments and therapies. Guests can also savor gourmet cuisine at the hotel's award-winning restaurant, which features a terrace overlooking the beautiful gardens.

With meticulous attention to detail and commitment to an unforgettable stay, The Royal Crescent Hotel & Spa is an ideal choice for luxury travelers.

The Bath Priory Hotel, Restaurant & Spa:

Located in a secluded setting, The Bath Priory Hotel, Restaurant & Spa is a sanctuary of serenity and luxury. Set within four acres of beautifully landscaped gardens, this boutique hotel offers a tranquil escape from the bustle of the city. The individually designed rooms and suites exude timeless elegance and comfort, while the hotel's renowned restaurant delights guests with creative, Michelin-starred cuisine made from locally sourced ingredients. The on-site spa offers a range of bespoke treatments, and guests can enjoy leisurely walks in the picturesque gardens or relax by the outdoor pool. The Bath Priory Hotel embodies a sense of refined sophistication that captivates discerning travelers.

Lucknam Park Hotel & Spa:

Situated just outside Bath in the idyllic Wiltshire countryside, Lucknam Park Hotel & Spa offers a luxurious retreat surrounded by breathtaking natural beauty. This five-star country house hotel combines Georgian charm with contemporary luxury, providing an enchanting blend of old-world elegance and modern amenities. The hotel features beautifully appointed rooms and suites, a Michelin-starred restaurant, and an array of leisure facilities, including a state-of-the-art spa, equestrian center, and tennis courts. Guests can immerse themselves in the estate's tranquility, explore the extensive grounds, or enjoy rejuvenating spa treatments. Lucknam Park Hotel & Spa promises an unforgettable escape into refined luxury.

The Abbey Hotel:

Located in the heart of Bath's historic center, The Abbey Hotel offers a stylish and contemporary take on luxury accommodation. This boutique hotel combines modern design with the city's rich heritage, creating a unique and captivating ambiance. The rooms and suites are elegantly appointed, with luxurious amenities and chic decor. The hotel's award-winning restaurant showcases a fusion of innovative flavors and locally sourced ingredients. At the same time, the rooftop bar provides a vibrant and stylish setting to enjoy panoramic views of the city. The Abbey Hotel's central location allows guests to easily explore Bath's attractions, including the Roman Baths and Bath Abbey, which are just a stone's throw away. With its modern sophistication and warm hospitality, The Abbey Hotel offers a contemporary luxury experience in the heart of Bath.

No.15 Great Pulteney:

No.15 Great Pulteney is a boutique hotel that exudes charm and character. Located on one of Bath's grandest streets, this Georgian townhouse hotel combines whimsical design with luxurious comfort. Each room and suite is individually decorated with eclectic furnishings, creating a unique and enchanting atmosphere. Guests can indulge in delectable cuisine at the hotel's restaurant, which showcases a creative menu inspired by local and seasonal ingredients. The hotel also boasts a spa and wellness center where guests can rejuvenate with various treatments and therapies. No.15 Great Pulteney offers a distinctive and memorable stay for those seeking elegance and whimsy.

Homewood:

Nestled amidst the rolling countryside just outside of Bath, Homewood is a luxury country retreat that offers a tranquil escape. This Georgian estate features elegantly designed rooms and suites, each with unique style and charm. Guests can unwind in the hotel's spa, which features a heated outdoor swimming pool, sauna, and steam room, or explore the beautiful gardens and surrounding woodlands. Homewood's restaurant showcases a menu celebrating locally sourced ingredients, providing a gastronomic journey through the region's flavors. With its idyllic setting and personalized service, Homewood offers a peaceful sanctuary for those seeking a luxurious countryside retreat.

The Pig Near Bath:

For a rustic and luxurious experience, The Pig near Bath is a hidden gem nestled in the Mendip Hills. This charming country house hotel boasts individually styled rooms with distinct characters and picturesque landscape views. The hotel's restaurant uses locally sourced and foraged ingredients, creating a menu showcasing the best of seasonal produce. Guests can explore the hotel's extensive kitchen garden, relax in the outdoor spa garden, or enjoy a cocktail in the cozy lounge. The Pig near Bath offers a unique and immersive luxury experience that combines the comforts of a country retreat with a farm-to-table culinary journey.

Bath's luxury hotels offer exceptional opulence, comfort, and personalized service, ensuring an unforgettable stay in this historic city. From the elegant Georgian townhouses to the tranquil countryside retreats, each hotel presents its unique charm and style. Whether you prefer the grandeur of a historic building, the contemporary allure of a boutique hotel, or the serenity of a country estate, Bath's luxury hotels cater to every discerning traveler's needs. Indulge in the finest accommodations, gourmet cuisine, and world-class spa facilities as you immerse yourself in this remarkable city's rich heritage and enchanting ambiance. A stay in one of Bath's luxury hotels promises a memorable and lavish experience that will leave you rejuvenated and longing to return.

MID-RANGE HOTELS AND BED AND BREAKFASTS

Bath is a captivating destination that attracts visitors from around the world. While luxury hotels offer unparalleled opulence, mid-range hotels, and bed and breakfasts provide a comfortable and charming alternative for budget-conscious travelers. In this chapter, we will explore a selection of mid-range accommodations in Bath, highlighting their unique features, convenient locations, and the warm hospitality they offer guests seeking a memorable and affordable stay.

The Windsor:

Located in the heart of Bath, The Windsor is a charming mid-range hotel that combines comfort with a touch of elegance. The hotel offers well-appointed rooms with modern amenities, ensuring a cozy and relaxing stay. The Windsor's central location makes it convenient for exploring Bath's attractions, including the Roman Baths and Bath Abbey. Guests can enjoy a complimentary breakfast each morning and unwind in the hotel's cozy lounge. With its friendly service and convenient amenities, The Windsor is an excellent choice for affordable accommodation without compromising quality.

The Ayrlington:

Situated in a Victorian townhouse, The Ayrlington is a delightful bed and breakfast that captures the essence of Bath's historic charm. The individually decorated rooms exude character and provide a comfortable retreat after a day of exploring the city. Guests can enjoy a freshly prepared breakfast in the elegant dining room, featuring a selection of locally sourced ingredients. The Ayrlington's tranquil garden offers a peaceful oasis, perfect for unwinding with a book or sipping tea. With its warm hospitality and attention to detail, The Ayrlington provides a memorable and affordable stay in Bath.

Brooks Guesthouse:

Brooks Guesthouse is a stylish and contemporary mid-range accommodation near the city center. This boutique guesthouse features tastefully designed rooms with modern amenities, including comfortable beds and en-suite bathrooms. The guesthouse also offers a communal lounge area where guests can relax and socialize. A highlight of Brooks Guesthouse is its hearty breakfast, which includes various options for different dietary preferences. The guesthouse's convenient location allows easy access to Bath's attractions, shops, and restaurants, making it an ideal choice for budget-conscious travelers seeking a trendy and comfortable stay.

The Griffin Inn:

The Griffin Inn is a charming bed and breakfast with a traditional English pub. The inn offers cozy rooms with comfortable furnishings and modern amenities. Guests can enjoy a hearty breakfast in the inn's dining area or indulge in traditional British pub fare for lunch or dinner. The Griffin Inn's idyllic location provides a peaceful retreat away from the city's hustle and bustle yet still within easy reach of Bath's attractions. With its warm and welcoming ambiance, The Griffin Inn offers a genuine taste of British hospitality.

Harington's Hotel:

Harington's Hotel is a boutique hotel in the heart of Bath's historic center. This Georgian townhouse hotel offers stylish and comfortable rooms uniquely decorated with modern amenities. The hotel's central courtyard provides a tranquil outdoor space where guests can relax and unwind. Harington's Hotel is known for its friendly and attentive service, ensuring every guest's pleasant and personalized experience. With its convenient location and affordable rates, Harington's Hotel is an excellent choice for those seeking centrally located and charming mid-range accommodation.

The Bath House Boutique Bed and Breakfast:

The Bath House Boutique Bed and Breakfast is a hidden gem in a quiet residential area, just a short walk from Bath's city center. This charming B&B offers individually styled rooms with contemporary and traditional designs. Guests can start their day with a delicious breakfast made with locally sourced ingredients, served in the elegant dining room. The B&B also features a cozy lounge area where guests can relax and unwind. The Bath House Boutique Bed and Breakfast pride itself on its warm and personalized service, ensuring guests feel welcome and well taken care of throughout their stay. With its peaceful location and attention to detail, this B&B offers a tranquil and affordable retreat in the heart of Bath.

The Old Mill Hotel:

Situated on the banks of the River Avon, The Old Mill Hotel offers a picturesque setting for a mid-range stay in Bath. Housed in a converted 18th-century mill, this hotel combines historic charm with modern comforts. The rooms are tastefully decorated and provide a comfortable sanctuary after a day of exploring the city. Guests can enjoy a meal at the hotel's restaurant, which features a riverside terrace, offering stunning views and a relaxing ambiance. The Old Mill Hotel's convenient location allows easy access to Bath's attractions, including the nearby Prior Park Landscape Garden. With its scenic surroundings and friendly service, The Old Mill Hotel offers a delightful and affordable stay.

The Roseate Villa Bath:

The Roseate Villa Bath is a boutique hotel in a stunning Georgian building near the city center. The hotel features beautifully appointed rooms and suites that blend contemporary and traditional elements. Guests can enjoy a sumptuous breakfast in the elegant dining room or relax in the lounge. The Roseate Villa Bath's attentive staff provides personalized service, ensuring a memorable and enjoyable stay. With its convenient location and stylish accommodations, this hotel offers a mid-range option for those seeking luxury without breaking the bank.

The Halcyon:

Located in a quiet residential area, The Halcyon is a charming bed and breakfast with a cozy and intimate atmosphere. The rooms are individually decorated, providing a unique and comfortable retreat. Guests can enjoy a hearty breakfast in the dining room or relax in the peaceful garden. Halcyon's friendly hosts always offer recommendations and assistance, ensuring a warm and personalized experience. With its homely ambiance and affordable rates, The Halcyon provides a delightful and welcoming stay in Bath.

The County Hotel:

The County Hotel is a budget-friendly option just a short walk from Bath's city center. The hotel offers comfortable and well-appointed rooms, providing a convenient base for exploring the city's attractions. Guests can start their day with a continental breakfast in the dining area before discovering Bath's cultural treasures. The County Hotel's friendly staff is always available to assist guests with inquiries or travel arrangements. With its affordable rates and convenient location, The County Hotel is a practical choice for budget-conscious travelers.

Mid-range hotels and bed and breakfasts in Bath offer a comfortable and charming alternative for travelers seeking affordability without compromising quality. From stylish boutique accommodations to cozy guesthouses, each establishment provides a unique experience that captures the essence of Bath's rich history and warm hospitality. Whether you prefer a central location, a tranquil retreat, or a riverside setting, these mid-range options cater to various preferences and budgets. Embrace these accommodations' comfort, charm, and personalized service as you explore the city's captivating attractions and immerse yourself in its vibrant culture. A stay in a mid-range hotel or bed and breakfast in Bath promises a delightful and affordable experience that will leave you with lasting memories of this remarkable city.

BUDGET-FRIENDLY ACCOMMODATIONS IN BATH

Bath is renowned for its luxurious hotels and charming bed and breakfasts. There are also plenty of budget-friendly accommodations that offer comfort, convenience, and affordability. To help you explore a selection of budget-friendly accommodations in Bath, highlighting their unique features, prime locations, and the value they provide to travelers seeking an affordable stay without compromising on quality, come along with me.

YHA Bath:

YHA Bath is a budget-friendly hostel that offers comfortable and affordable accommodations for travelers on a tight budget. Located just a short walk from the city center, the hostel provides dormitory-style and private rooms with shared bathrooms. The communal areas, including the lounge and self-catering kitchen, create a friendly and sociable atmosphere where guests can mingle with fellow travelers. YHA Bath also offers a range of amenities, such as free Wi-Fi, laundry facilities, and a 24-hour reception. With its central location and budget-friendly rates, YHA Bath is ideal for backpackers and budget-conscious travelers.

Bath Backpackers:

Bath Backpackers is another popular choice for budget travelers seeking affordable accommodations in the city's heart. This friendly and welcoming hostel offers dormitory-style and private rooms, providing options for solo travelers and groups. Bath Backpackers features a communal kitchen where guests can prepare meals and a cozy lounge area to relax and socialize. The central hostel allows easy access to Bath's main attractions, including the Roman Baths and Bath Abbey. With its affordable rates and laid-back atmosphere, Bath Backpackers is an excellent choice for travelers looking to make the most of their budget while exploring the city.

Redcar Hotel:

Situated in a charming Georgian townhouse, the Redcar Hotel offers affordable accommodations with a touch of elegance. The hotel provides comfortable rooms with en-suite bathrooms, ensuring a pleasant and convenient stay. Guests can start their day with a continental breakfast served in the dining area, and the hotel's friendly staff is always on hand to provide recommendations and assistance. The Redcar Hotel's central location allows easy access to Bath's attractions, shops, and restaurants, making it an excellent choice for budget-conscious travelers looking for a convenient and affordable base in the city.

Oldfields House:

Oldfields House is a charming bed and breakfast that offers budget-friendly accommodations in a tranquil residential area of Bath. The guesthouse features cozy and comfortable rooms with en-suite or shared bathrooms, providing options for different budgets. Guests can enjoy a delicious breakfast in the dining room, which includes a selection of freshly prepared dishes using locally sourced ingredients. Oldfields House also offers free Wi-Fi and complimentary parking, adding value for money. With its peaceful location and warm hospitality, this bed and breakfast offers travelers a relaxing and affordable retreat.

Travelodge Bath Central:

Travelodge Bath Central offers affordable accommodations in a convenient location for those seeking a budget-friendly hotel chain. The hotel features clean and comfortable rooms with en-suite bathrooms, providing a comfortable stay at a reasonable price. Guests can enjoy a hearty breakfast at the hotel's onsite restaurant or explore the nearby cafes and eateries. The Travelodge Bath Central's prime location allows easy access to Bath's main attractions, including the Thermae Bath Spa and Pulteney Bridge. With its affordable rates and convenient amenities, this hotel is an excellent choice for budget-conscious travelers seeking a comfortable and well-located accommodations.

Holiday Inn Express Bath:

Holiday Inn Express Bath offers affordable accommodations with a range of amenities for a comfortable stay. The hotel features modern and well-appointed rooms that provide a cozy and relaxing environment. Each room has comfortable beds, a work desk, a flat-screen TV, and complimentary Wi-Fi, ensuring a convenient stay for guests. The hotel also offers a complimentary breakfast buffet to start the day.

Holiday Inn Express Bath guests can also use the hotel's additional amenities, including a 24-hour front desk, a business center, and a fitness center. The friendly and attentive staff is always available to assist with inquiries or requests, ensuring guests have a pleasant and hassle-free experience.

The hotel's prime location is another highlight. Situated just a short distance from the city center, guests can easily explore Bath's famous attractions, such as the Roman Baths, Bath Abbey, and the Royal Crescent. The hotel is also conveniently located near public transportation options, making it easy to explore the wider area.

The Windsor Guest House:

The Windsor Guest House offers affordable and comfortable accommodations in a charming Victorian building. The guest house features well-appointed rooms with modern amenities, including en-suite bathrooms, flat-screen TVs, and complimentary Wi-Fi. Each room is tastefully decorated, creating a welcoming and cozy atmosphere for guests.

A highlight of the Windsor Guest House is the delicious morning breakfast. Guests can enjoy a variety of options, including cooked breakfast, continental choices, and vegetarian alternatives, ensuring there's something to suit every palate.

The guest house's location is another advantage. It is within walking distance of Bath's city center, allowing guests to easily explore the city's attractions, shops, and restaurants. The friendly and attentive staff is also available to provide recommendations and assistance, ensuring guests make the most of their time in Bath.

Z Hotel Bath:

Z Hotel Bath offers affordable and stylish accommodations in the city's heart. The hotel features compact yet well-designed rooms that maximize space and comfort. Each room has a comfortable bed, an en-suite shower, a flat-screen TV, and complimentary Wi-Fi. The modern design and thoughtful amenities create a contemporary and inviting atmosphere.

Guests at Z Hotel Bath can also take advantage of the hotel's complimentary breakfast buffet, which includes a selection of hot and cold options. The hotel's central location lets guests easily explore Bath's attractions, including the Roman Baths and Thermae Bath Spa.

Bath Paradise House Hotel:

Bath Paradise House Hotel offers budget-friendly accommodations in a Georgian townhouse, providing a charming and authentic experience. The hotel features comfortable rooms with en-suite bathrooms, ensuring a pleasant and convenient stay. Guests can enjoy a continental breakfast in the elegant dining room overlooking the beautiful gardens.

The hotel's location is another highlight. It is just a short walk from Bath's city center, allowing guests to easily explore the city's attractions, shops, and restaurants. The friendly and knowledgeable staff always provides recommendations and assistance, ensuring guests have a memorable stay.

The Griffin Inn:

The Griffin Inn is a traditional pub with budget-friendly accommodations located in the picturesque village of Bathampton, just a short drive from Bath's city center. The inn offers comfortable and cozy rooms with en-suite bathrooms, providing a peaceful retreat after a day of exploration.

Guests at The Griffin Inn can also indulge in delicious meals at the pub's onsite restaurant, which serves various traditional British dishes and local specialties. The cozy atmosphere and friendly staff create a welcoming and relaxed ambiance.

The inn's location allows guests to enjoy the charm of Bathampton while still being within easy reach of Bath's city center. The surrounding countryside also offers opportunities for scenic walks and outdoor activities.

Bath offers a range of budget-friendly accommodations that provide travelers comfort, convenience, and affordability. Whether you choose a budget-friendly hostel, a charming bed, breakfast, or a well-located hotel, these accommodations ensure you can enjoy all Bath offers without breaking the bank. From comfortable rooms to friendly staff, these establishments strive to provide a pleasant stay while keeping costs affordable.

Exploring Bath on a budget doesn't mean compromising quality or missing out on the city's rich history and stunning architecture. With these budget-friendly accommodations, you can experience the charm of Bath without sacrificing comfort or convenience. Whether you're a solo traveler, a couple, or a family, options are available to suit your needs and preferences.

Moreover, staying in budget-friendly accommodations allows you to allocate more of your travel budget to other experiences, such as exploring Bath's museums and galleries, indulging in local cuisine, or joining guided walking tours. By choosing affordable accommodations, you can make the most of your visit to Bath while keeping your travel expenses in check.

It's important to note that budget-friendly accommodations may have limitations compared to their higher-priced counterparts. For example, you may find shared facilities, smaller rooms, or fewer amenities. However, their value in terms of cost savings and prime locations makes them an excellent choice for budget-conscious travelers who prioritize exploring the city over luxurious accommodations.

Planning and reserving your stay in advance, especially during peak travel seasons, is advisable when booking budget-friendly accommodations. This ensures you secure the best rates and availability for your desired dates. Additionally, reading reviews and checking the establishment's website or booking platforms can provide insights into the quality of service and facilities.

In conclusion, Bath offers a range of budget-friendly accommodations that cater to travelers seeking affordability without compromising comfort or convenience. Whether you choose a hostel, a be,d and breakfast, or a budget hotel, these establishments provide a comfortable and welcoming environment, allowing you to enjoy all Bath offers while staying within your travel budget. So pack your bags, plan your itinerary, and get ready to embark on an unforgettable adventure in the beautiful and historic city of Bath.

CHAPTER 7: DAY TRIPS FROM BATH

STONEHENGE

Bath is a beautiful city full of history and culture, but if you want to explore beyond the city limits, you can take plenty of great day trips from Bath. One of the most popular destinations is Stonehenge, one of the world's most famous prehistoric monuments.

Stonehenge is 35 miles north of Bath, making it a convenient and easy day trip. The site consists of a circle of massive stones, some weighing up to 50 tons, erected over 4,500 years ago. The purpose of the stones remains a mystery, but they are believed to have had religious or ceremonial significance.

There are several ways to visit Stonehenge from Bath. One option is to take a guided tour, which can be booked through various companies. These tours typically include transportation to and from Stonehenge, as well as a knowledgeable guide who can provide insights into the history and significance of the site. Some tours may also include visits to other nearby attractions, such as the medieval city of Salisbury or the ancient hill fort of Old Sarum.

Another option is to rent a car and drive yourself to Stonehenge. The journey takes around an hour, and ample parking is available on site. This option allows you to explore the site at your own pace and visit other nearby attractions.

Once you arrive at Stonehenge, you can take a guided tour of the site or explore independently. There is also a visitor center that features exhibits on the history and significance of Stonehenge, as well as a cafe and gift shop.

Regardless of how you visit Stonehenge, it will be a fascinating and memorable experience. The site's ancient history and mysterious origins continue to captivate visitors from all over the world.

Wells

Another excellent day trip option from Bath is the city of Wells, located just 20 miles south of the city. Wells is known for its stunning cathedral, which dates back to the 12th century and is considered one of the most beautiful in England.

In addition to the cathedral, Wells also has a charming historic center with cobbled streets and picturesque architecture. The city's marketplace has a weekly farmers' market where you can sample local foods and crafts.

Other notable attractions in Wells include the Bishop's Palace and Gardens, which date back to the 13th century and feature stunning gardens and medieval architecture. The Wells and Mendip Museum is also worth a visit, with exhibits on the local area's history.

The city is easily accessible from Bath by car or public transportation. If you take the bus, catch Number 174 from Bath's bus station, which runs hourly throughout the day.

Cheddar Gorge and Caves

For nature lovers, a trip to Cheddar Gorge and Caves is a must-see day trip from Bath. The gorge is a natural wonder, with towering limestone cliffs and stunning views of the surrounding countryside.

The caves in Cheddar Gorge are also a highlight, with guided tours available to explore the underground caverns and learn about the area's geology and history. The Cheddar Gorge Cheese Company is another popular attraction where you can sample and purchase local cheeses.

Cheddar Gorge is 25 miles southwest of Bath and can be reached by car or public transportation. If you take the bus, catch Number 376 from Bath's bus station, which runs several times daily.

Longleat Safari Park

Longleat Safari Park is a fun and exciting day trip option from Bath for families with children. The park features a drive-through safari, where you can see animals such as lions, tigers, giraffes, and monkeys up close from the comfort of your car. The safari park is set on a sprawling estate and offers a unique opportunity to observe exotic wildlife in their natural habitats.

In addition to the safari, Longleat also boasts a stunning stately home with beautiful gardens open to the public. You can explore the grand rooms of the house, marvel at the impressive architecture, and learn about the history of the estate.

The park offers a range of other attractions, including adventure playgrounds, boat rides, and animal encounters. Regular events and shows, such as bird of prey displays and sea lion presentations, keep visitors entertained throughout the day.

Longleat is approximately 30 miles east of Bath and can be reached by car in under an hour. Alternatively, bus and train options are available for those who prefer not to drive. The park has ample parking facilities, and tickets can be purchased online in advance to save time.

Glastonbury

Just a short drive from Bath, Glastonbury is a mystical and enchanting town steeped in history and folklore. Known for its connections to King Arthur, Glastonbury Abbey, and the annual Glastonbury Festival, this town has a unique and spiritual atmosphere that attracts visitors worldwide.

Glastonbury Abbey is one of the town's main attractions. With its ruins dating back to the 7th century, it is said to be the burial place of King Arthur and Queen Guinevere. Exploring the abbey grounds immerses you in this ancient site's rich history and legends.

Another notable landmark in Glastonbury is the Tor, a conical hill offering panoramic countryside views.

Climbing to the top of the Tor is a popular activity for visitors, and it provides a sense of peace and tranquility.

Glastonbury is known for its eclectic mix of shops, cafes, and alternative therapies. The town is a hub for spirituality, alternative lifestyles, and holistic healing, with many independent stores offering crystals, books on esoteric subjects, and various forms of healing and divination.

Driving is best to reach Glastonbury from Bath, as public transportation options are limited. The journey takes around 50 minutes, and several parking areas are available in the town center.

BRISTOL

Bristol is a fantastic choice if you're looking for a vibrant and cosmopolitan day trip. Located just 13 miles west of Bath, Bristol is a thriving city with a rich maritime history, a vibrant arts scene, and a wide range of attractions to explore.

One of the city's most iconic landmarks is the Clifton Suspension Bridge, designed by Isambard Kingdom Brunel. The bridge spans the Avon Gorge and offers breathtaking city and surrounding countryside views. Walking across the bridge is a must-do activity for visitors to Bristol.

Bristol is also home to several excellent museums and art galleries. The Bristol Museum and Art Gallery houses diverse artwork and historical artifacts. At the same time, the SS Great Britain allows visitors to step back in time and explore the world's first great ocean liner.

For those interested in street art, a visit to Bristol would only be complete with exploring the works of the internationally renowned graffiti artist Banksy. The city is full of murals and stencils; even guided tours are available that take you to some of his most famous pieces.

In addition to its cultural offerings, Bristol is also a fantastic city for shopping and dining. The city center has various shops, from high-street brands to independent boutiques and a wide selection of restaurants, cafes, and bars.

Bristol is easily accessible from Bath by train, with regular direct services between the two cities. The journey takes around 15 minutes, making it a convenient and hassle-free day trip option.

Bristol offers something for everyone, whether you're interested in history, art, shopping, or simply soaking up the vibrant atmosphere of a bustling city. From its historic harbor and maritime heritage to its modern street art and cultural scene, there is no shortage of things to see and do.

If you're interested in maritime history, visiting the SS Great Britain is necessary. Step aboard this iconic ship, designed by Isambard Kingdom Brunel, and explore its fascinating history as the world's first great ocean liner. The interactive exhibits and displays bring the ship's past to life, offering a glimpse into the lives of the passengers and crew.

Bristol's historic harbor area, Bristol Harbourside, is another must-visit destination. Stroll along the waterfront, admire the beautifully restored ships, and explore the M Shed museum, which showcases the city's rich history and heritage.

Art enthusiasts will be delighted by Bristol's thriving street art scene. Banksy, one of the world's most renowned street artists, hails from Bristol, and his thought-provoking and often controversial works can be found throughout the city. Join a guided street art tour to discover some of the best pieces and learn about the artists behind them.

Bristol is also known for its vibrant music and arts scene. The city boasts numerous live music venues, theaters, and galleries where you can catch performances ranging from intimate gigs to large-scale productions. Check the local listings to see what events are happening during your visit.

When it comes to shopping, Bristol doesn't disappoint. The city center has many shops, from high-street brands to independent boutiques and vintage stores. Whether looking for fashion, homeware, or unique gifts, you'll find plenty of options to satisfy your retail cravings.

When it's time to refuel, Bristol offers a diverse culinary scene that caters to all tastes and budgets. From traditional British pubs serving hearty meals to trendy eateries offering international cuisine, you'll find many dining options to suit your preferences. Remember to sample local specialties, such as a Bristolian cider or a tasty Bristol cream tea.

In conclusion, a day trip to Bristol from Bath is a fantastic opportunity to explore a vibrant and culturally rich city.

Whether you're interested in history, art, shopping, or simply soaking up the lively atmosphere, Bristol has something for everyone. With its excellent transport links and diverse attractions, Bristol is a must-visit destination that will leave you wanting to return for more. So, plan your day trip, pack your bags, and get ready to discover the delights of Bristol, just a short journey from Bath.

THE COTSWOLDS

The Cotswolds is a region of unparalleled beauty and charm, making it an ideal day trip destination from Bath. The Cotswolds offer a glimpse into rural England with its rolling hills, quaint villages, and idyllic landscapes. The Cotswolds has it all, whether you're seeking tranquility, outdoor adventures, or a taste of traditional village life.

The Cotswolds is renowned for its stunning scenery, characterized by gentle hills and lush meadows dotted with charming honey-colored stone villages. Exploring these villages is like stepping back in time, with their well-preserved historic architecture, thatched cottages, and village greens. Each place has unique characters and attractions, from the bustling market towns of Chipping Campden and Stow-on-the-Wold to the picturesque villages of Bibury and Bourton-on-the-Water.

One of the most iconic attractions in the Cotswolds is the village of Castle Combe, often called the "prettiest village in England." Its enchanting streets, lined with centuries-old cottages and flower-filled gardens, evoke a sense of timeless beauty. Stroll through the village, visit the medieval church, and enjoy a traditional pub lunch in one of the charming local establishments.

For nature enthusiasts, the Cotswolds offers ample opportunities to explore its breathtaking landscapes. The region is crisscrossed by footpaths and bridleways, making it a paradise for hikers and cyclists. Routes suit all abilities and interests, from gentle walks along the River Windrush to more challenging hikes up the Cotswold escarpment. Pack a picnic and take advantage of the numerous scenic spots.

History buffs will be delighted by the Cotswolds' rich heritage. The region is home to several historic houses and castles that provide a glimpse into its past. Sudeley Castle, located near Winchcombe, is a magnificent Tudor castle surrounded by stunning gardens. Explore its royal connections and learn about its fascinating history, including its association with Queen Katherine Parr, the last wife of Henry VIII.

Another notable historic site is Blenheim Palace, located on the edge of the Cotswolds near Woodstock. This grand stately home, a UNESCO World Heritage site, is the birthplace of Sir Winston Churchill and boasts breathtaking architecture, formal gardens, and a fascinating exhibition on Churchill's life and legacy. Take a guided tour of the palace, stroll through the landscaped gardens, and enjoy the tranquility of the surrounding parkland.

Food and drink lovers will find plenty to enjoy in the Cotswolds. The region is known for its local produce, artisanal food products, and traditional pubs. Sample delicious Cotswold cheeses, indulge in locally sourced meats and vegetables, and wash it down with a pint of locally brewed ale. Many villages have quaint tea rooms and country pubs where you can experience the region's warm hospitality and culinary delights.

To fully immerse yourself in the Cotswolds experience, consider joining a guided tour. Local guides can provide valuable insights into the area's history, culture, and hidden gems. They can take you off the beaten path, sharing stories and anecdotes that bring the Cotswolds to life.

Getting to the Cotswolds from Bath is relatively easy, with several transportation options. Guided tours and day trips from Bath are readily available if you prefer a hassle-free journey. These tours often include transportation, expert guides, and visits to multiple villages and attractions, allowing you to maximize your time in the Cotswolds.

Alternatively, if you prefer to travel independently, you can take a train or bus to the larger towns in the region, such as Moreton-in-Marsh or Cheltenham, and then explore the surrounding villages by local bus or taxi. The Cotswolds is well-connected by public transportation, making it accessible for day-trippers.

Once in the Cotswolds, there are countless activities and sights to enjoy. One popular activity is visiting the area's various gardens and parks. Hidcote Manor Garden, for example, is a world-renowned garden known for its intricately designed outdoor spaces, beautiful flowers, and stunning vistas. The garden is divided into "outdoor rooms," each with a unique character and design. Take a stroll through the park, soak in the peaceful ambiance, and admire the artistry of the landscape.

Another delightful garden to explore is the Painswick Rococo Garden, which showcases the playful and ornate Rococo style. This hidden gem features winding paths, follies, and exotic and rare plants. It's a place where whimsy and beauty combine, offering a truly unique and enchanting experience.

Visiting the impressive Sudeley Castle is a must for those interested in history and architecture. This historic castle boasts stunning gardens, a fascinating exhibition on its royal connections, and the resting place of Queen Katherine Parr. Explore the castle's rich history, wander through the award-winning gardens, and enjoy the tranquil surroundings.

The Cotswolds is also home to numerous charming market towns where you can immerse yourself in the local culture and experience traditional village life. Cirencester, known as the "Capital of the Cotswolds," is a bustling market town with a rich Roman history. Explore its historic streets, visit the Corinium Museum to learn about the town's Roman past, and browse the local shops and markets.

Burford, often called the "Gateway to the Cotswolds," is another must-visit town. Its picturesque High Street has historic buildings, traditional pubs, and independent shops. Take a stroll along the river, soak in the atmosphere of this quintessential Cotswold town, and perhaps enjoy a cream tea in one of the charming tea rooms.

If you want a quintessential Cotswold village experience, head to Bourton-on-the-Water. Known as the "Venice of the Cotswolds," this village is characterized by its low stone bridges that span the tranquil River Windrush. Explore the charming streets, visit the model village, and enjoy a picnic by the river.

Outdoor enthusiasts will find plenty of opportunities for activities such as hiking, cycling, and horse riding in the Cotswolds. The region is crisscrossed with an extensive network of footpaths and bridleways that wind through the countryside, offering breathtaking views and peaceful surroundings. Whether you prefer a stroll or a more challenging hike, there are routes to suit all abilities and fitness levels.

The Cotswolds is also known for its vibrant arts and crafts scene. Explore the local galleries and craft shops to discover unique and handmade treasures. From pottery and ceramics to textiles and jewelry, the Cotswolds is a haven for art lovers and collectors.

Consider indulging in the local cuisine to make the most of your day trip to the Cotswolds. The region is known for its delicious and hearty traditional dishes, such as Cotswold lamb, Gloucestershire sausages, and locally sourced cheeses. Many villages have charming pubs and tearooms where you can enjoy a leisurely meal or afternoon tea, complete with homemade scones and clotted cream.

In conclusion, a day trip to the Cotswolds from Bath is a delightful way to experience rural England's beauty, history, and charm. From the quaint villages and historic landmarks to the stunning landscapes and delicious local cuisine, the Cotswolds offers visitors a rich and diverse experience. Whether you rest in history, nature, art, or simply soaking up the peaceful countryside atmosphere, the Cotswolds has something for everyone.

To ensure a successful day trip to the Cotswolds, here are a few practical tips:

- Plan your itinerary: The Cotswolds covers a wide area, so it's essential to plan your itinerary. Decide which villages, attractions, and activities to prioritize and allocate your time accordingly. Consider the distances between locations and factor in travel time.

- Choose your transportation: If you prefer a hassle-free experience, joining a guided tour or hiring a private driver is convenient. These options offer the advantage of expert guides who can provide valuable insights and handle the logistics. Alternatively, public transportation is viable if you prefer to travel independently. Trains and buses connect Bath to various towns in the Cotswolds, allowing you to explore the region at your own pace.

- Check opening times and admission fees: Some attractions in the Cotswolds may have limited opening hours or require bookings, especially during peak tourist seasons. Check the official websites of the places you plan to visit to confirm their opening times and any admission fees. This will help you optimize your time and avoid disappointment.

- Dress appropriately: The Cotswolds is known for its changeable weather, so it's advisable to dress in layers and be prepared for rain or sunshine. Wear comfortable shoes, especially if you plan to walk or hike, as some paths may be uneven or muddy.

- Bring a map or guidebook: While many villages in the Cotswolds are well-signposted, having a map or guidebook can help navigate the smaller, less touristy areas. It can also provide additional information about each place you visit's history, architecture, and attractions.

- Support local businesses: The Cotswolds has many independent shops, cafes, and restaurants. Make an effort to support these local businesses by purchasing souvenirs, trying traditional dishes, or enjoying a meal in a local eatery. This contributes to the local economy and allows you to experience the authentic flavor of the region.

- Respect the environment and local communities: As you explore the Cotswolds, you must be mindful of the environment and the communities you encounter. Follow designated footpaths and avoid damaging or disturbing wildlife and vegetation. Dispose of any waste responsibly and respect the privacy and tranquility of residential areas.

Remember, a day trip to the Cotswolds from Bath is just a glimpse into the region's beauty and charm. If time permits, consider extending your visit or planning a longer getaway to immerse yourself in the Cotswold experience fully. With its timeless villages, stunning landscapes, and rich heritage, the Cotswolds offers an unforgettable journey into the heart of rural England.

OTHER NEARBY ATTRACTIONS

When visiting the beautiful city of Bath, several captivating attractions are nearby that make for excellent day trips. Whether you're interested in exploring historic sites, natural wonders, or picturesque towns, the region surrounding Bath offers many possibilities. Here are some of the major nearby attractions worth considering for a memorable day trip.

1. Bristol: Located just a short distance from Bath, the vibrant city of Bristol is a fantastic destination for a day trip. Bristol boasts a rich maritime heritage and is famous for its iconic Clifton Suspension Bridge, designed by Isambard Kingdom Brunel. Explore the historic harbor area, visit the award-winning SS Great Britain, and wander through the vibrant street art scene that Bristol is renowned for. The city also offers excellent shopping, dining, and cultural experiences, including world-class museums and galleries.

2. Wells: A short drive from Bath will lead you to the charming city of Wells, often called the smallest city in England. It is known for its magnificent cathedral, Wells Cathedral, which features stunning Gothic architecture and a breathtaking interior. Explore the picturesque streets lined with independent shops and cafés, and visit the Bishop's Palace, a medieval palace surrounded by a tranquil moat. Don't miss the chance to wander through the vibrant Wells Market, which takes place twice a week and offers a wide variety of local produce and crafts.

3. Longleat Safari Park: For a unique and exciting day out, head to Longleat Safari Park, approximately 30 minutes from Bath. It is one of the oldest safari parks outside of Africa and offers an incredible opportunity to get close to a wide range of exotic animals. Take a safari drive-through, where you can see lions, tigers, giraffes, and many other fascinating creatures. Explore the stunning stately home, Longleat House, and its beautifully landscaped

gardens. There are also various other attractions, including boat rides, a maze, and a jungle cruise.

4. Avebury: Step back in time and visit the ancient stone circles of Avebury, located a short drive from Bath. This Neolithic henge monument is one of Europe's largest and most impressive and even more significant in scale than Stonehenge. Take a walk around the stone circles, marvel at the standing stones, and soak in the mystical atmosphere of this UNESCO World Heritage Site. The nearby Avebury Manor and Museum offer further insights into the history and significance of the area.

5. Cheddar Gorge and Caves: Nature enthusiasts will be captivated by the natural wonder of Cheddar Gorge and Caves, located within an hour's drive from Bath. Explore the dramatic limestone gorge with its towering cliffs and winding footpaths, offering stunning panoramic views. Venture into the awe-inspiring caves to discover ancient stalactites and stalagmites. The area also provides opportunities for hiking, rock climbing, and caving

adventures, making it a haven for outdoor enthusiasts.

6. Glastonbury: Known for its mystical and spiritual associations, Glastonbury is a fascinating town that attracts visitors from all walks of life. Visit Glastonbury Tor, a hill with panoramic views and an intriguing history intertwined with Arthurian legends. Explore the ruins of Glastonbury Abbey, said to be the final resting place of King Arthur and Guinevere. Discover the unique shops and cafes in the town center, offering everything from New Age books to handmade crafts. Glastonbury also hosts several festivals annually, including the renowned Glastonbury Festival of Contemporary Performing Arts.

7. Lacock: Fans of period dramas and historical architecture will delight in visiting Lacock, a quintessentially English village around 30 minutes from Bath. This beautifully preserved village has been a filming location for numerous movies and TV series, including "Harry Potter" and "Downton

Abbey." Stroll through the picturesque streets with charming stone cottages and immerse yourself in the timeless atmosphere. Visit Lacock Abbey, a medieval nunnery turned country house boasting stunning architecture, tranquil gardens, and fascinating history. Take advantage of the opportunity to indulge in a traditional cream tea at one of the cozy tearooms in the village.

8. Salisbury: Just a short drive from Bath, Salisbury is a historic city with many attractions. The centerpiece is Salisbury Cathedral, known for its magnificent spire, medieval architecture, and the best-preserved original copy of the Magna Carta. Explore the charming streets lined with timber-framed buildings, visit the Salisbury Museum to delve into the city's history, or take a leisurely walk along the picturesque River Avon. Nearby, you'll find the mysterious prehistoric monument of Stonehenge, a UNESCO World Heritage Site and one of the most iconic landmarks in the world.

9. Bradford-on-Avon: For a delightful and tranquil day trip, visit the charming town of Bradford-on-Avon, located just a short distance from Bath. This quaint town is brimming with history and boasts well-preserved architecture, including the stunning 14th-century Bradford-on-Avon Tithe Barn. Take a leisurely walk along the picturesque Kennet and Avon Canal, visit the Saxon Church of St. Laurence, and explore the narrow streets with independent shops and cafes. The surrounding countryside offers scenic walking and cycling trails, providing a peaceful retreat from the bustle of the city.

10. Corsham: A hidden gem in the region, Corsham is a delightful town with a rich history and architectural charm. Explore the grandeur of Corsham Court, an Elizabethan mansion with impressive gardens, and discover the fascinating underground quarries known as the Corsham Tunnels, which served as a secret military facility during World War II. Wander through the town

center and admire the historic buildings, browse the antique shops, and relax in one of the cozy pubs or tearooms.

When embarking on a day trip from Bath to these nearby attractions, consider the following tips:

- Check transportation options: Research the available transportation options for each destination, whether by car, train, or bus. Determine the most convenient and time-efficient method of travel and plan accordingly. Public transportation is often a suitable choice, allowing you to relax and enjoy the scenery without worrying about parking or navigating unfamiliar roads.

- Check opening hours and admission fees: Before visiting any attractions, check their opening hours and fees. Some sites may have seasonal variations in their schedules or require bookings. Planning ensures you maximize your day trip and avoid disappointment.

- Pack essentials: Depending on the nature of your day trip, pack essentials such as comfortable walking shoes, weather-appropriate clothing, a water bottle, snacks, and a camera to capture the beautiful moments. Consider bringing a guidebook or map for reference and information on the attractions you'll be visiting.

- Allocate time wisely: Consider the distance between Bath and each destination and the estimated time required to explore and appreciate each attraction. Allow for flexibility in your itinerary, as unexpected discoveries or longer-than-anticipated visits may occur.

- Immerse yourself in local culture: Embrace the unique atmosphere and local culture of each destination you visit. Engage with the locals, sample regional cuisine, and explore the shops and markets to experience the charm and character of the area thoroughly.

Whether you delve into history, marvel at natural wonders, or soak in the atmosphere of quaint towns, the nearby attractions from Bath offer a diverse range of experiences for a fulfilling day trip. Each destination has distinctive charm and interests, from Bristol's vibrant city to Glastonbury's mystical town. Take the opportunity to explore historic landmarks, immerse yourself in nature, and indulge in the local culture and cuisine.

As you plan your day trips, consider the transportation logistics, such as using public transportation or renting a car. Public transportation can be a convenient option, mainly if you prefer to sit back and enjoy the scenic views without the hassle of driving and parking. However, renting a car may be a better choice if you prefer more flexibility and the ability to explore off-the-beaten-path locations.

Before setting off, check the opening hours and admission fees of the attractions you plan to visit. This will help you optimize your time and avoid unexpected closures or fees. Additionally, consider the distance and travel time between each destination, allowing for a comfortable pace and enough time to experience each place fully.

When packing for your day trips, bring essentials such as comfortable walking shoes, weather-appropriate clothing, a water bottle, and snacks. Having a camera or smartphone handy is also essential to capture the memories of your day trips. Consider bringing a guidebook or downloading a travel app to learn more about each destination's history, culture, and highlights.

To make the most of your day trips, immerse yourself in the local culture and embrace the unique atmosphere of each place. Engage with the locals, start conversations, and seek their recommendations for hidden gems or local experiences. Whether trying traditional dishes, browsing local markets, or attending festivals or events, immersing yourself in the local culture will enrich your day trip experiences.

Remember to allocate your time wisely, allowing for a balance between exploration and relaxation. While trying and seeing everything in one day is tempting, it's important to savor each moment and not rush through the attractions. Take your time to appreciate the historical significance of sites, explore the natural beauty of the surroundings, and create lasting memories.

Lastly, embrace the spirit of adventure and be open to unexpected discoveries. Sometimes the most memorable moments of a day trip come from serendipitous encounters or spontaneous detours. Allow yourself to be flexible with your itinerary and let the day unfold naturally.

In conclusion, the region surrounding Bath offers many fascinating day trip options, each with its unique attractions and experiences. Whether you explore the historic city of Wells, marvel at the ancient stones of Avebury, or soak in the natural beauty of Cheddar Gorge, each day's trip promises an enriching and memorable adventure. Plan your day trips carefully, immerse yourself in the local culture, and embrace the spirit of discovery. With these tips in mind, your day trips from Bath will be filled with captivating experiences and a deeper appreciation for the region's rich heritage and natural wonders.

CHAPTER 7: PRACTICAL INFORMATION FOR VISITORS

BEST TIME TO VISIT BATH

The city of Bath, with its rich history, stunning architecture, and relaxing thermal spas, is a captivating destination to visit throughout the year. However, like any other travel destination, the timing of your visit can significantly impact your experience. To make the most of your trip to Bath, it's essential to consider the best time to visit based on weather, crowds, and special events. This chapter will help you navigate the seasons and choose the perfect time for your Bath adventure.

Spring (March to May):
Spring in Bath is a beautiful time when nature awakens, and the city comes alive with vibrant blooms and

blossoms. The temperatures rise, ranging from mild to warm, making outdoor activities and exploration comfortable. This season is perfect for leisurely walks in the parks and gardens, such as the stunning Prior Park Landscape Garden and the Royal Victoria Park. The city is less crowded than in the summer, allowing you to enjoy the attractions without long queues. Spring also brings several events, including the Bath Comedy and Bath Festival, featuring music, literature, and art. It's an ideal time for those who appreciate milder weather, blossoming landscapes, and cultural events.

Summer (June to August):

Summer is the peak tourist season in Bath due to its warm and pleasant weather. The temperatures range from mild to hot, making it perfect for exploring the city's outdoor attractions, such as the Roman Baths and the iconic Pulteney Bridge. The long daylight hours provide ample time for sightseeing, and the city's parks and green spaces, like Sydney Gardens and Alexandra Park, are ideal for picnics and relaxation. However, be prepared for larger crowds and long queues at popular attractions, especially during weekends and school holidays. The summer months also bring a vibrant festival atmosphere, with events like the Bath International Music Festival and the Jane Austen Festival. If you don't mind the crowds and enjoy the buzz of summer activities, this is the best time to visit Bath.

Autumn (September to November):
Autumn in Bath is a magical time as the city transforms into a tapestry of rich colors with changing leaves. The temperatures gradually cool down, creating a pleasant atmosphere for outdoor exploration. The autumn foliage creates a picturesque backdrop, especially in parks like Alexandra Park and Bathwick Hill. This season is also an excellent time to visit the nearby countryside and enjoy scenic walks in the Cotswolds or the Avon Valley. The city experiences fewer crowds than in summer, allowing for a more peaceful and relaxed visit. Autumn is also a great time for food enthusiasts, as it coincides with the Great Bath Feast, a celebration of local food and drink. If you

prefer a quieter visit and appreciate the beauty of autumn landscapes, this season is ideal for your trip to Bath.

Winter (December to February):

Winter in Bath offers a unique charm with its festive atmosphere and cozy ambiance. The temperatures are colder, ranging from chilly to mild, and occasional snowfall can add a touch of magic to the city's historic streets. The main attractions, such as the Roman Baths and Bath Abbey, are less crowded, allowing you to explore more leisurely. The city's Christmas Market, held from late November to early December, is a highlight of the winter season, offering a wide range of festive treats, crafts, and entertainment. The Thermae Bath Spa becomes even more enticing during the colder months with its warm thermal waters. Winter is an excellent time for relaxation, spa treatments, and enjoying cozy pubs and tearooms. If you're a fan of winter charm, festive markets, and a quieter atmosphere, visiting Bath during winter will provide a unique and enchanting experience.

In summary, the best time to visit Bath depends on your preferences and what you want to experience during your trip. Each season in Bath has its unique offerings, whether it's the blooming flowers of spring, the vibrant summer festivals, the colorful foliage of autumn, or the festive charm of winter.

Consider the following factors to help you decide the best time to visit:

1. Weather: Spring and autumn are ideal if you prefer milder temperatures and a comfortable climate for outdoor activities. Summers can be warm and pleasant, perfect for exploring Bath's outdoor attractions. Winter brings colder temperatures but adds a cozy and festive atmosphere to the city.

2. Crowds: If you prefer to avoid large crowds and long queues at popular attractions, consider visiting during the quieter spring or autumn seasons.

Summers are the busiest, with higher tourist numbers, while winters are generally less crowded.

3. Events and Festivals: Bath hosts various events and festivals throughout the year. If you're interested in cultural celebrations, music festivals, or specific events like the Jane Austen Festival or the Bath Christmas Market, plan your visit accordingly to coincide with these festivities.

4. Budget: Consider the cost of accommodation and flights, which can vary depending on the season. Off-peak seasons like spring and autumn may offer more affordable options than peak summer.

5. Nature and Scenery: If you're interested in experiencing the beauty of nature, such as blooming flowers in spring or colorful foliage in autumn, plan your visit accordingly. Each season offers a different backdrop for exploring Bath's parks, gardens, and nearby countryside.

Ultimately, the best time to visit Bath is subjective and depends on your personal preferences. Whether you visit during the bustling summer months, the serene beauty of autumn, or the festive charm of winter, Bath will undoubtedly captivate you with its history, architecture, culture, and natural surroundings. Plan your visit accordingly, and prepare to be enchanted by this remarkable city.

CURRENCY AND MONEY EXCHANGE

When planning a trip to a foreign country like Bath, England, it's essential to understand the local currency and plan money exchange. Proper knowledge and preparation will ensure a smooth and hassle-free financial experience during your visit.

The Currency: The official currency of the United Kingdom, including Bath, is the British Pound Sterling (£). It is divided into 100 pence (p). The pound sterling is represented by the symbol "£" and is commonly called "quid" in informal language. Notes come in denominations of £5, £10, £20, and £50, while coins come in denominations of 1p, 2p, 5p, 10p, 20p, 50p, £1, and £2.

Currency Exchange Options:

1. Banks: Banks are the most reliable and secure places to exchange currency. Central banks in Bath, such as Barclays, HSBC, Lloyds, and NatWest, provide currency exchange services. They offer competitive exchange rates but keep in mind that they may charge commission or service fees. You should check with your local bank in advance for their exchange rates and any associated fees.

2. Currency Exchange Offices: Bath has several currency exchange offices and bureaux de change. These establishments specialize in foreign exchange and offer competitive rates.

3. ATMs: Automated Teller Machines (ATMs) are widely available throughout Bath, making withdrawing cash in the local currency convenient. ATMs usually offer competitive exchange rates; you can use your debit or credit card to withdraw money. However, remember that your bank may

charge fees for international withdrawals, so it's advisable to check with your bank beforehand.

4. Prepaid Travel Cards: Another option is to use prepaid travel cards, such as those offered by central banks or currency exchange providers. These cards allow you to load money onto them in advance and use them like debit cards while traveling. They often offer competitive exchange rates, which you can use for purchases and ATM withdrawals. However, be aware of any fees for obtaining or using these cards.

Currency Tips and Considerations:

❖ Inform Your Bank: Before traveling to Bath, inform your bank or credit card company about your travel plans. This ensures they won't flag your transactions as suspicious when you use your cards abroad. It's also good to inquire about any fees or restrictions that may apply to your overseas cards.

❖ Cash vs. Cards: While most businesses in Bath accept card payments, it's still advisable to carry some cash for small purchases, transportation, or places that may not accept cards. Some establishments, mainly smaller shops, cafes, or market vendors, may prefer cash payments. Always keep your cash secure and be cautious of pickpocketing in crowded areas.

❖ Exchange Rates: Exchange rates can fluctuate, so it's wise to keep an eye on them and consider exchanging money when the rates are favorable. Various websites and mobile apps provide real-time exchange rate information to help you make informed decisions.

❖ Local Spending: When making purchases or paying for services in Bath, ensure you know of any additional charges or fees. Some establishments may charge a transaction fee for using a card, especially for smaller amounts. Always check your receipt for any additional charges.

❖ Tipping: Tipping in Bath is customary but not obligatory. Leaving a gratuity of around 10% to 15% in restaurants is expected if you're satisfied with the service. However, checking the bill first is always good, as some restaurants include a service charge. In hotels, it's customary to leave a small tip for staff who provide exceptional services, such as the concierge or housekeeping.

❖ Safety and Security: When exchanging money or using ATMs, it's essential to prioritize your safety and be aware of your surroundings. Choose well-lit and secure locations for currency exchange or ATM withdrawals. Avoid displaying large amounts of cash, and keep your cards and PINs safe.

❖ Currency Conversion Apps: Consider using currency conversion apps on your smartphone for quick and easy reference to exchange rates. These apps can help you calculate the approximate value of your money in the local currency and ensure you're getting a fair deal.

❖ Exchanging Leftover Currency: If you have leftover British pounds at the end of your trip, you can exchange them back to your local currency at currency exchange offices or banks. Remember that exchange rates for converting back to your original currency may differ from when you initially exchanged your money.

Finally, understanding the currency and money exchange options in Bath will help you navigate the financial aspects of your trip with confidence. Whether you exchange cash at banks, use ATMs, or opt for prepaid travel cards, be mindful of exchange rates and associated fees. Inform your bank about your travel plans, carry a mix of cash and cards, and be aware of local customs and tipping practices. By following these tips and considerations, you can ensure a smooth and hassle-free financial experience during your visit to Bath, allowing you to focus on enjoying the rich history, stunning architecture, and relaxing thermal spas the city offers.

SAFETY TIPS FOR VISITORS

Safety is a top priority for any visitor to a new destination, and Bath is no exception. While Bath is generally a safe city, it's always wise to take precautions to ensure a smooth and worry-free visit. Whether exploring the historical sites, enjoying the local culture, or simply strolling through the charming streets, these safety tips will help you make the most of your time in Bath while keeping yourself and your belongings secure.

1. Stay Aware of Your Surroundings: One of the most important safety tips is to stay alert and aware of your surroundings. Be observant of the people around you, especially in crowded areas or busy tourist attractions. Avoid distractions like excessive mobile phone use or headphones that may limit your awareness.

2. Secure Your Belongings: Keep your belongings secure to prevent theft or loss. Invest in a secure and sturdy bag or backpack with a zipper closure. Keep your wallet, passport, and other valuables in

secure inner pockets. Avoid carrying large amounts of cash or wearing expensive jewelry that may attract unnecessary attention.

3. Use Reliable Transportation: Opt for reputable, licensed public transportation or taxi services. Pre-book your transportation through trusted companies. If you're using ride-hailing apps, ensure that the driver and vehicle details match the information provided in the app. If you're walking at night, stick to well-lit and populated areas.

4. Be Cautious of Scams: Like any popular tourist destination, Bath may have individuals attempting various scams. Be cautious of people approaching you with unsolicited offers or trying to engage you in conversation to distract you. Avoid giving personal information or money to strangers, and be skeptical of deals that seem too good to be true.

5. Stay on Designated Paths and Trails: Bath offers beautiful parks, gardens, and countryside areas for visitors to explore. When venturing into these areas, stay on designated paths and trails. Straying off

marked paths may lead to treacherous terrain or disturb protected wildlife areas. Follow any signs or guidelines provided in these natural areas.

6. Keep Emergency Contacts Handy: It's essential to have emergency contact numbers readily available during your trip. Make a note of the local emergency services number 999 in the UK. Save the contact information for your accommodation, embassy, and any local contacts you may have. Having a copy of your identification documents stored securely is also a good idea.

7. Respect Local Laws and Customs: Familiarize yourself with the local laws and customs of Bath before your visit. Respect cultural norms and traditions, and adhere to any rules or regulations at historical sites, museums, or religious places. Follow instructions from authorities and respect any signage or guidance provided for your safety.

8. Use Hotel Safes: If your accommodation offers in-room safes, utilize them to store your valuable items when you're not using them. This includes

passports, extra cash, and any essential documents. If your hotel doesn't have in-room safes, inquire about secure storage options for your valuables at the front desk.

9. Stay Hydrated and Take Breaks: Bath is a beautiful city with much to explore, but taking care of your physical well-being while sightseeing is essential. Stay hydrated by carrying a water bottle and drinking regularly, especially on hot days. Take breaks when needed, rest in shaded areas, and avoid overexertion to prevent heat-related illnesses or fatigue.

10. Trust Your Instincts: Finally, trust your instincts and intuition. If a situation or place feels unsafe or uncomfortable, remove yourself from it. Your safety and well-being should always be your top priority. Contact local authorities or seek assistance from trusted sources if you have concerns.

11. Plan Ahead: Before your trip, research and familiarize yourself with the areas you plan to visit in

Bath. Understand the city's layout, identify potentially unsafe neighborhoods, and plan your itinerary accordingly. This will help you avoid getting lost or finding yourself in unfamiliar or hazardous surroundings.

12. Travel Insurance: It's always recommended to have travel insurance that covers medical expenses, trip cancellation, and lost or stolen belongings. Having adequate insurance provides peace of mind and financial protection in unexpected situations.

13. Stay Connected: Ensure you have reliable communication while in Bath. Carry a charged mobile phone with you at all times, and save important contact numbers, including your hotel, local emergency services, and your embassy or consulate. If you're traveling with a group or partner, establish a meeting point in case you get separated.

14. Public Transport Safety: When using public transportation in Bath, be cautious and aware of your surroundings. Keep your belongings close to

you, and be mindful of pickpockets in crowded areas. If you're taking a taxi, choose licensed and reputable taxi services, and avoid accepting rides from unmarked or unauthorized vehicles.

15. Respect Local Customs: Bath has a rich history and cultural heritage. Respect the local customs, traditions, and dress codes, especially when visiting religious sites or participating in cultural events. Familiarize yourself with any specific cultural norms to avoid inadvertently offending the locals.

16. Emergency Preparedness: Familiarize yourself with the nearest hospitals, medical facilities, and pharmacies in Bath. Carry a basic first-aid kit with band-aids, pain relievers, and necessary prescription medications. If you have specific medical conditions or allergies, wear a medical alert bracelet or carry a card with relevant information.

17. Stay in Well-Lit Areas: When walking around Bath, particularly at night, stick to well-lit and populated areas. Avoid dimly lit streets or shortcuts through

secluded areas. If possible, travel with a companion, as there is safety in numbers.

18. Be Mindful of Local Laws: Observe and respect the local laws and regulations in Bath. Familiarize yourself with the legal drinking age, smoking restrictions, and specific public behavior rules. Breaking local laws can have serious consequences, so being a responsible visitor is essential.

19. Stay Hydrated and Sunscreen: Bath can experience warm weather during the summer months. Drink plenty of water to stay hydrated, especially if you spend significant time outdoors. Apply sunscreen regularly to protect your skin from the sun's harmful rays.

20. Trust Your Intuition: Finally, trust your instincts. If you feel uncomfortable or sense a potentially unsafe situation, remove yourself. Your intuition is a valuable tool for assessing the safety of your surroundings. Feel free to seek help or advice from local authorities or trusted individuals.

Following these tips can enhance your safety and peace of mind while visiting Bath. It's always better to be proactive and take precautions than to encounter unfortunate situations. Enjoy exploring Bath's rich history, stunning architecture, and cultural delights while keeping yourself safe and secure. Safety should always be a priority when traveling, and Bath is no exception. By following these safety tips, you can ensure a smooth and worry-free visit to this beautiful city.

Remember, these safety tips will enhance your experience and ensure your well-being while visiting Bath. By staying vigilant, being aware of your surroundings, and taking necessary precautions, you can enjoy your time in this beautiful city with peace of mind.

USEFUL PHRASES IN ENGLISH

English is a widely spoken language worldwide, and a basic understanding of useful phrases can significantly enhance your travel experience. Whether you're visiting Bath for leisure or business, here are some essential English phrases that will help you navigate through various situations and communicate effectively:

1. Greetings and Basic Expressions:
   - Hello / Hi - A common way to greet someone.
   - Good morning/afternoon/evening - Greetings based on the time of day.
   - How are you? - A friendly way to inquire about someone's well-being.
   - Thank you / Thanks - Expressing gratitude.
   - You're welcome - A response to express that something is not a problem or inconvenience.
   - Excuse me / Pardon me - Used to get someone's attention or to apologize for interrupting.

- I'm sorry - Apologizing for any mistake or inconvenience.

2. Asking for Help:
   - Can you help me, please? - Seeking assistance or information.
   - Where is...? - Asking for directions to a specific location.
   - How can I get to...? - Inquiring about the best way to reach a particular place.
   - Do you speak English? - Checking if someone can communicate in English.
   - I need help understanding - Expressing confusion or difficulty in understanding.
   - Can you repeat that, please? - Asking someone to repeat what they said.

3. Ordering Food and Drinks:
   - I would like... - Indicate your food or drink preference.

- Could I have...? - A polite way to request something.
- The bill, please - Asking for the check in a restaurant or café.
- Do you have any vegetarian options? - Inquiring about vegetarian food choices.
- I'm allergic to... - Informing the waiter about food allergies or dietary restrictions.

4. Shopping:

- How much does it cost? - Asking for the price of an item.
- Do you have this in a different size/color? - Inquiring about product availability.
- Can I try it on? - Asking to test or try on a piece of clothing.
- Can I have a receipt, please? - Requesting a receipt for your purchase.

5. Transportation:

- Where is the nearest bus/train station? - Asking for the location of public transportation.
- How much is a ticket to...? - Inquiring about the cost of a ticket to a specific destination.
- When does the next bus/train leave? - Asking about the departure time of the next bus or train.
- Is this seat taken? - Checking if a seat is already occupied.

6. Emergency Situations:
   - Help! - Calling for assistance in an emergency.
   - I need a doctor/hospital - Expressing the need for medical aid.
   - My bag has been stolen - Reporting a theft or loss of personal belongings.
   - Where is the nearest police station? - Asking for the location of the nearest police station.

7. Polite Phrases:

- Please - Used to make a request or show politeness.
- Excuse me - A polite way to get someone's attention or to apologize.
- May I...? - Seeking permission for something.
- Could you please...? - A polite way to ask someone to do something.

8. Common Courtesies:
   - Goodbye / Bye – Farewell, greetings.
   - Have a lovely day/evening - Wishing someone a pleasant day or evening.
   - Nice to meet you - Expressing pleasure in meeting someone for the first time.
   - Take care - Wishing someone to stay safe.

9. Asking for Directions:
   - Can you tell me how to get to...? - Seeking directions to a specific place.
   - Is it far from here? - Inquiring about the distance to a particular destination.

- Which way should I go? - Asking for guidance on the correct path.

10. Making Small Talk:
    - What's your name? - Initiating a conversation by asking someone's name.
    - Where are you from? - Showing interest in someone's place of origin.
    - What do you do for a living? - Inquiring about someone's profession or occupation.
    - Do you have any recommendations? - Asking for suggestions or advice on places to visit or things to do.

11. Expressing Preferences:
    - I like... - Sharing your preferences or interests.
    - I prefer... - Stating a stronger preference for something.
    - I'm interested in... - Indicating your interest in a particular topic or activity.

- I'm not a fan of... - Expressing that something is not your liking.

12. Discussing the Weather:
    - It's sunny/cloudy/rainy today - Commenting on the current weather conditions.
    - It's hot/cold outside - Expressing the temperature outside.
    - What's the forecast for tomorrow? - Inquiring about the weather forecast for the next day.

13. Talking about Time and Dates:
    - What time is it? - Asking for the current time.
    - What day is it today? - Inquiring about the current day of the week.
    - When is your birthday? - Showing interest in someone's birthday.

14. Expressing Gratitude and Politeness:

- That's very kind of you - Showing appreciation for someone's kindness.
- I appreciate it - Expressing sincere gratitude.
- Excuse me, but... - Politely interrupting a conversation or seeking attention.

15. Making Apologies:
   - I'm sorry for the inconvenience - Apologizing for causing inconvenience.
   - I apologize for my mistake - Taking responsibility for an error.
   - Please forgive me - Seeking forgiveness for a mistake or misunderstanding.

16. Offering Help:
   - Can I assist you with anything? - Offering your assistance to someone in need.
   - Would you like some help? - Extending a helping hand to someone.

17. Expressing Emotions:

- I'm happy/sad/excited - Sharing your emotional state.
- I feel... - Expressing your emotions or thoughts.

18. Confirming Information:
- To clarify... - Seeking clarification or confirmation on a certain point.
- So, if I understand correctly... - Summarize to ensure understanding.

19. Negotiating:
- Is there any room for negotiation? - Inquiring about the possibility of negotiation.
- Can we work out a better price? - Requesting a better deal or discount.

20. Saying Goodbye:
- Take care of yourself - Wishing someone well as you part ways.

- It was nice talking to you - Expressing enjoyment in the conversation.
- Have a safe trip - Wishing someone a safe journey.

21. Asking for Recommendations:
- What are the must-see attractions in Bath? - Seeking advice on the top sights to visit.
- Can you recommend a good restaurant nearby? - Asking for suggestions on where to eat.
- Are there any local events happening this week? - Inquiring about upcoming events or festivals.

22. Expressing Admiration:
- This place is stunning/beautiful/amazing! - Expressing admiration for the surroundings.
- I'm impressed by the architecture/history/culture here - Showing appreciation for the city's unique features.

23. Engaging in Conversation:

- What do you like most about Baths? - Initiating a conversation about locals' favorite aspects of the city.
- Tell me about the local traditions and customs - Showing interest in the cultural practices of the region.
- Do you have any insider tips for exploring Bath? - Seeking local insights and hidden gems.

24. Seeking Assistance with Technology:

- Can you help me connect to the Wi-Fi? - Asking for assistance with internet access.
- My phone battery is low. Is there a charging point nearby? - Inquiring about a place to charge electronic devices.

25. Expressing Concern:

- I'm feeling a bit lost - Expressing concern about being unsure of one's location.

- Is this area safe at night? - Asking for information about the safety of a particular neighborhood.

26. Complimenting the Locals:
    - You have a lovely city - Complimenting the residents on their beautiful city.
    - The people here are so friendly and welcoming - Praising the locals for their hospitality.

27. Talking about Hobbies and Interests:
    - Do you have any recommendations for outdoor activities? - Seeking suggestions for outdoor adventures.
    - Are there any good bookstores/art galleries/museums in the area? - Inquiring about specific interests.

28. Inquiring about Local Transportation:

- How often do the buses/trains run? - Asking about the frequency of public transportation.

- Are there any bike rental services available in Bath? - Inquiring about bike rental options.

29. Discussing Sports and Entertainment:

- Are there any sports events happening in the city? - Inquiring about local sporting events.

- What are the popular leisure activities here? - Asking about recreational pursuits enjoyed by locals.

30. Showing Appreciation:

- I've had a wonderful time in Bath - Expressing gratitude for a memorable experience.

- I appreciate your help - Showing appreciation for someone's assistance.

By familiarizing yourself with these useful English phrases, you'll be better equipped to navigate various situations and communicate effectively during your visit to Bath. Don't be afraid to practice these phrases and engage with the locals—it's a great way to immerse yourself in the culture and make meaningful connections.

Remember, learning a few basic English phrases can go a long way in communicating effectively and creating a positive impression. Practice these phrases, be bold, and use them in Bath. Most importantly, be patient and open-minded, as locals will appreciate your efforts to

Remember also that practice is critical to improving your English communication skills. Use these phrases in your daily interactions and be open to learning from the locals. The more you engage with the language, the more confident you will become. Enjoy your time in Bath and embrace the opportunity to connect with people from different walks of life through the power of language.

CONCLUSION:

FINAL THOUGHTS ON BATH

Bath is a captivating city that offers a rich tapestry of history, culture, stunning architecture, and rejuvenating thermal spas. Its ancient origins as a Roman settlement, followed by its transformation during the Georgian era, have left an indelible mark on the cityscape and created a unique atmosphere that continues attracting visitors worldwide.

From exploring the ancient Roman Baths to marveling at the grandeur of Georgian architecture, there are great landmarks and attractions to discover in Bath. The city's museums and art galleries provide insights into its past and showcase impressive collections of art and artifacts. The vibrant theater scene and numerous festivals and events ensure that there is always something exciting happening in Bath.

Regarding cuisine, Bath offers a delectable array of traditional British food and local specialties. From hearty pub fare to fine dining experiences, visitors can indulge in various culinary delights. The city's charming cafes and cozy pubs provide the perfect setting to relax and savor the flavors of Bath.

As you explore Bath, you'll immerse yourself in its architectural splendor. The diverse architectural styles, from Roman to Georgian to modern, create a visual feast for the eyes. Walking tours offer an excellent way to discover the city's hidden gems and uncover its architectural treasures.

One of the highlights of a visit to Bath is the opportunity to unwind and pamper yourself in the city's top spas and thermal baths. The healing waters have been revered for centuries, and today, they offer a sanctuary for relaxation and rejuvenation. Whether you immerse yourself in the historic Roman Baths or indulge in a luxurious spa experience, Bath's thermal spas provide a blissful escape from the hustle and bustle of everyday life.

In terms of accommodations, Bath caters to every budget and preference. Many options are available, from luxury hotels with elegance and sophistication to cozy bed and breakfasts with a more intimate experience. You can expect warm hospitality and exceptional service regardless of where you stay.

Bath's location also makes it an ideal base for exploring the surrounding areas. Day trips to iconic attractions like Stonehenge and the picturesque Cotswolds are easily accessible, allowing visitors to expand their horizons and delve deeper into the beauty of the English countryside.

When planning your visit to Bath, it's essential to consider the best time to go. The city's mild climate and year-round appeal make it a destination that can be enjoyed anytime. However, the summer months of June to August offer longer days and pleasant temperatures, making it a popular time for tourists. Spring and autumn also present a lovely time to visit, with fewer crowds and beautiful seasonal landscapes.

As a visitor to Bath, you must familiarize yourself with practical information such as currency and money exchange, safety tips, and proper English phrases. Being prepared will ensure a smooth and enjoyable experience throughout your stay.

In conclusion, visiting Bath is an immersive journey through time and a feast for the senses. The city offers a unique blend of history, culture, relaxation, and entertainment, from ancient Roman roots to Georgian elegance and modern vibrancy. Whether you're exploring its iconic landmarks, indulging in local cuisine, or immersing yourself in its thermal spas, Bath is sure to leave an indelible impression and create memories to last a lifetime. So, pack your bags and embark on an unforgettable adventure to the picturesque city of Bath.

PLANNING YOUR NEXT VISIT TO BATH.

Bath, with its rich history, stunning architecture, and relaxing thermal spas, is a city that captivates visitors worldwide. Whether you're a history enthusiast, a culture lover, a foodie, or simply seeking a rejuvenating getaway, Bath has something to offer everyone. Here are some critical aspects of planning your next visit to Bath, ensuring you make the most of your time in this picturesque city.

1. Determining the Best Time to Visit: Choosing the right time to visit Bath is crucial to ensure an enjoyable experience. The city's mild climate and year-round appeal make it a destination that can be visited anytime. However, there are certain factors to consider. The summer months of June to August offer longer days, pleasant temperatures, and a bustling atmosphere with various events and festivals. Spring and autumn present beautiful seasonal landscapes, fewer crowds, and more affordable accommodation options. Winter,

although colder, offers a unique charm with its festive decorations and the opportunity to enjoy the thermal spas in a cozy setting.

2. Duration of Your Stay: Deciding on your visit to Bath depends on your interests and the activities you wish to engage in. While exploring the city's highlights in a couple of days is possible, consider allocating at least three to four days to fully immerse yourself in Bath's history, culture, and attractions. This will allow ample time to visit the iconic landmarks, indulge in the thermal spas, sample the local cuisine, and take day trips to nearby attractions.

3. Creating an Itinerary: To make the most of your time in Bath, it's advisable to create an itinerary. Start by identifying the key attractions you wish to visit, such as the Roman Baths, the Royal Crescent, and the Bath Abbey. Allocate sufficient time to explore each site and consider guided tours or audio guides for a more enriching experience. Additionally, plan visits to the city's museums and

art galleries, attend live performances at the theaters and set aside time for relaxation at the thermal spas.

4. Accommodation Options: Bath offers various accommodations to suit different budgets and preferences. Luxury hotels provide opulent surroundings, excellent amenities, and impeccable service. Mid-range hotels and bed and breakfasts offer a comfortable stay with personalized touches and a homely ambiance. Some affordable guesthouses and hostels offer budget-conscious travelers basic amenities and a convenient base for exploring the city. When choosing accommodation, consider location, proximity to attractions, and access to public transportation.

5. Transportation: Getting to Bath is relatively easy, with good transportation links from major cities in the UK. If arriving by train, the Bath Spa railway station is conveniently located in the city center. Several parking options are available for those traveling by car, including public car parks and on-street parking. Within Bath, the city center is

compact and best explored on foot. However, if you prefer alternative modes of transportation, local buses, and taxis are readily available. Cycling is also popular, and the city offers bike rental services.

6. Dining and Culinary Experiences: Bath boasts a vibrant food scene, offering various dining options to satisfy every palate. From traditional British cuisine to international flavors, the city is a haven for foodies. Explore the local specialties such as Bath buns, Sally Lunn buns, and locally produced cheeses. Indulge in a traditional afternoon tea experience or savor a meal in one of Bath's many excellent restaurants. For a more immersive experience, consider joining a food tour or cooking class to learn about the local culinary traditions.

7. Exploring Beyond Bath: While Bath offers abundant attractions and activities, it's worth considering exploring the surrounding areas to enhance your visit. Day trips from Bath provide an opportunity to discover nearby attractions and experience the beauty of the English countryside.

Some popular day trip options include:

- Stonehenge: Just a short distance from Bath, Stonehenge is an iconic and mysterious UNESCO World Heritage Site. Marvel at the ancient stone circle and contemplate its enigmatic history. Guided tours are available to provide insights into the significance of this ancient monument.

- The Cotswolds: Known for its picturesque villages, rolling hills, and charming countryside, it is a must-visit destination. Take a leisurely drive through the scenic landscapes, visit quaint villages like Castle Combe and Bourton-on-the-Water, and immerse yourself in the quintessential English countryside.

- Longleat Safari Park: Located near Bath, Longleat Safari Park offers a thrilling wildlife experience. Take a safari drive and encounter majestic animals such as lions, tigers, giraffes, and elephants. Explore the stately home and beautiful gardens, and enjoy various family-friendly attractions and activities.

- Bristol: Just a short distance from Bath, the vibrant city of Bristol is worth a visit. Explore its rich maritime heritage at the SS Great Britain, stroll along the historic harborside, and discover the vibrant street art scene. Bristol also offers a range of museums, galleries, and shopping opportunities.
- Glastonbury: Known for its mystical and spiritual connections, Glastonbury is a unique destination. Visit Glastonbury Abbey, climb Glastonbury Tor for panoramic views, and explore the quirky shops and cafes in the town. Take the chance to learn about the legends and myths associated with the area.

When planning your day trips, consider the logistics of transportation, as well as the opening hours and ticket availability for each attraction. It's advisable to book guided tours or purchase tickets in advance to secure your spot and make the most of your time.

8. Shopping and Souvenirs: Bath offers a diverse shopping experience, ranging from high-end boutiques to independent shops and markets. Explore the bustling streets of Milsom Street, Walcot Street, and Stall Street, where you'll find a mix of fashion, jewelry, homeware, and unique local crafts. Remember to visit the Bath Christmas Market if you're visiting during the festive season, where you can browse a wide range of stalls offering handmade crafts and delicious food. For souvenirs, consider items that reflect the city's heritage, such as Roman-themed memorabilia, locally produced beauty products, or unique artworks inspired by Bath's architecture. Bath's markets, including the Guildhall and Green Park Station, are great places to find local produce, artisanal goods, and vintage treasures.

9. Cultural Etiquette: When visiting Bath, it's essential to be aware of cultural etiquette to ensure a respectful and enjoyable experience. Respect the local customs and traditions, and be mindful of the

city's heritage. When visiting religious sites like Bath Abbey, dress modestly and observe specific rules or guidelines. It's also essential to be considerate of others when using public spaces, such as parks, restaurants, and transportation. Follow local norms, such as queuing patiently, using polite language, and respecting personal space. Bath is a welcoming and inclusive city, and embracing these cultural considerations will contribute to a positive interaction with the local community.

10.   Final Thoughts: In conclusion, planning your next visit to Bath involves considering various factors to ensure a memorable and fulfilling experience. From choosing the best time to visit and creating an itinerary to exploring beyond the city and immersing yourself in the local culture, Bath has much to offer. Whether seeking history, relaxation, culinary delights, or outdoor adventures, Bath caters to diverse interests and preferences.

By carefully planning your visit, you can make the most of your time in Bath and ensure that you take advantage of the city's highlights. Consider the best time to visit based on weather, events, and crowd levels. Determine the duration of your stay to allow ample time to explore Bath's attractions and indulge in its unique experiences.

Choosing suitable accommodation is essential for a comfortable and convenient stay. Whether you opt for luxury hotels, mid-range options, or budget-friendly accommodations, consider location, amenities, and proximity to key attractions.

Transportation in Bath primarily centers around walking, but public transportation options such as buses and taxis are available. If you plan on exploring the surrounding areas, renting a car or joining guided tours can provide convenient transportation solutions.

When it comes to dining, Bath offers a diverse culinary scene. There's something for every palate, from traditional British dishes to international cuisines. Take the chance to sample local specialties and indulge in afternoon tea or dining experiences unique to Bath.

Beyond the city limits, day trips from Bath allow you to explore nearby attractions such as Stonehenge, the Cotswolds, Bristol, and Glastonbury. These excursions offer an opportunity to experience the beauty of the English countryside and immerse yourself in the region's history and culture.

As a visitor, it's essential to be mindful of cultural etiquette and respect the local customs and traditions. Bath has a rich heritage, and being considerate and respectful can enhance your interactions with the local community.

Lastly, remember to plan for shopping and souvenirs. Bath offers a range of shopping experiences, from high-end boutiques to charming markets. Take the opportunity to purchase unique souvenirs that reflect the city's character and heritage.

In conclusion, planning your next visit to Bath involves carefully considering various factors. Planning your itinerary, selecting suitable accommodations, exploring day trip options, and embracing the local culture can create a truly memorable and fulfilling experience in this captivating city. Bath's rich history, stunning architecture, and welcoming atmosphere make it a destination worth exploring, and with proper planning, you can ensure that your visit exceeds your expectations. So, start planning your next trip to Bath and get ready to immerse yourself in the charm and beauty of this remarkable city.

THE END

Printed in Great Britain
by Amazon

25528750R00155